RAFAEL E. LÓPEZ-CORVO

The Traumatic Loneliness of Children

First published in 2020 by
Free Association Books

Copyright © 2020 Rafael E. López-Corvo

The author's rights are fully asserted. The rights of
Rafael E. López-Corvo to be identified as the author of this work
has been asserted by him in accordance with the
Copyright, Designs and Patents Act 1988

A CIP Catalogue of this book is available from
the British Library

ISBN: 978-1-91138-337-6

All rights reserved; no part of this publication may be reproduced,
stored in a retrieval system, or transmitted, in any form or by
any means, electronic, mechanical, photocopying, recording or
otherwise, without the prior written permission of the publisher.
Nor be circulated in any form of binding or cover other than that
in which it is published and a similar condition including this
condition being imposed on the subsequent purchaser.

Typeset by
Typo•glyphix
www.typoglyphix.co.uk

Cover design by
Candescent

Printed and bound in the UK

CONTENTS

Preface						vii

Chapter I
THE THEORY: 'PRE-CONCEPTUAL TRAUMAS'		1

Chapter II
THE 'TRAUMATISED STATE' IS STRUCTURED
FOLLOWING CHILDREN'S EPISTEMOLOGY		23

Chapter III
HOW CHILDREN THINK				43

Chapter IV
TRAUMATISED STATE AND ITS COMPULSION TO
REPEAT, AS A FORM OF DEFENCE			52

Chapter V
LONELINESS IS IN THE HEART OF
PRE-CONCEPTUAL TRAUMAS			62

Chapter VI
THE 'TRAUMATIC TRAP'				70

Chapter VII
VENGEFUL HOPE VS. RENUNCIATION HOPE		84

CONTENTS

Chapter VIII
EXCESS OF MOTHER AND ABSENCE OF FATHER, LONELINESS AND THE PHANTASY OF THE 'FECAL PHALLUS' — 111

Chapter IX
LONELINESS, FEELING OF 'NON-EXISTENCE', AND THE NEED OF A 'RESCUER' — 126

Chapter X
THE 'RESCUER' AS THE UNCONSCIOUS SOLUTION TO LONELINESS — 138

Chapter XI
LONELINESS AND THE OEDIPUS COMPLEX OR PARENTS AS 'RESCUERS' — 155

Chapter XII
WHY SELF-ENVY? — 164

Chapter XIII
LONELINESS IN A MAN BORN WITH A DISLOCATED SHOULDER: 'A WILD THOUGHT IN SEARCH OF A THINKER' — 180

References — 201
Index — 0

To my children,
Alex, Vane and Joa,
as well as my grandchildren,
Ashley, Adrian, Evan and Isabel.

ACKNOWLEDGEMENTS

I am very grateful to Ana Milagros López-Corvo for her unconditional help organising this book, as well as Kristen Hahn, for her wonderful review of the manuscript. Finally, I feel extremely indebted to Alice Solomons, my editor at Free Association Books, for her magnificent help and guidance.

PREFACE

The question is not so much if there is life after death, the question is more about if there is life before death.
— Osho

Every new arrival on this planet is faced with the task of mastering the Oedipus complex.
— Sigmund Freud (1905)

What progress, you ask, have I made? I have begun to be a friend to myself. That was indeed a great benefit; such a person can never be alone. You may be sure that such a man is a friend to all mankind.
— Seneca, Letters from a Stoic

When parents understand the universe where children dwell, the world will change!

*

It will be absolutely impossible to investigate psychopathology in adults, without taking into account children's epistemology, not because, as many have expressed, psychoanalysis is only interested in the past, but because, as Bion once stated, 'we are merely concerned with the past that is always repeating in the present'. The knowledge that the loneliness a child once experienced will always be echoed in the adult's emotional life, is quite familiar. Mexican Nobel Prize-winning writer, Octavio Paz (1997), in his book "The Labyrinth of Solitude", refers in sensible and beautiful prose to memories about his own childhood loneliness; reminiscences that could perhaps be considered as an expression of his own pre-conceptual trauma. He wrote the following:

> ...there is a coming and going of people who pass by the side of the bundle[1] without stopping. The bundle cries. For centuries cries and nobody hears it. He is the only one who hears his cry. He has gone astray in a world that is, at the same time, familiar and remote, intimate and indifferent...

And further on

> ...Endless instant: to hear oneself cry in the middle of universal deafness...the feeling has never been erased, and never will be. It is not a wound, it is a hole. When I think of myself, I touch it: as I sense it, I feel it. Alien always and always present, never leaves me, presence without body, mute, invisible, perpetual witness of my life. He does not speak to me, but sometimes I hear what his silence says to me: ...you discovered your absence, your hole: you discovered yourself. You already know: you are dearth and search. [p. 5][2]

**

I have given a transcendental importance to the presence of what I had referred to as the "Pre-conceptual trauma", or the trauma that takes place very early in life, in all existing human beings,

---

[1] He referred to himself as the "bundle".
[2] I am using Octavio Paz's Spanish version, because this quotation, that appears in its Prologue, is not present in the English translation of 1961.

which I will describe in detail in Chapter I. There is another question to consider: why is it possible to estimate the life span of any animal, but it is rather difficult to guestimate the life expectancy of a human being? I believe the difference hinges on the fact that animals, their behaviour and way of living, are structurally determined by rigid biological scripts, which we refer to as instincts. There is little room for improvisations and their behaviour will always follow the specific patterns determined by their drives. Humans, on the other hand, being bestowed by Nature with *consciousness* and self-awareness, have the aptitude and capacity to regulate their life on their own accord, rising above their genes and modifying their manners, a freedom that leads to narcissistic arrogance and to possible distancing from the regular pathways of Nature, often resulting – for instance – in unfair and cruel demands made by parents on their children. While animals, on the other hand, by being pure nature, lack the aptitude to derail themselves from those paths, and will always remain predictable and faithful to the direction of their genes and drives. In simple words, if an animal's life span is *phylogenetic*, humanity is *ontogenetic*. Humans are seriously influenced by pre-conceptual traumas resulting from parents' unpredictability, which does not exist in animals. At the same time, 'repetition compulsion' (the appellation Freud provided to the mechanism responsible for the continuous replication of pre-conceptual traumas) within the 'traumatised state' takes over the 'non-traumatised state' and controls our adult mind. By controlling the mind, the traumatised state will unconsciously introduce logics based on the child's epistemology, which will obviously smear, interfere, and disturb the adult's logical judgement. I believe that such interference determines the way we think and act, inducing states of confusion, anxiety, depression, and so on, which not only regulates our everyday form of living, but will eventually determine our life span. In comparison with the past, the current increment of life expectancy in humans, is much increased at the present time in comparison with the past, thanks to better therapeutic methods, such as new drugs and more sophisticated healing procedures; however, it is also possible that the greater understanding parents have now in relation to child rearing, thanks to a better knowledge of child psychology, may also diminish parents' cruelty, unfairness, and strict demands made on their children, thereby reducing children's sense of isolation and loneliness.

* * *

The work of Rene Spitz (1945) with 'primary deprivation' in small children, as well as Harlow's (1958) studies on monkeys, and Bowlby's[3] (1980, 1988) research on separation, evidenced the significance of the presence of a 'loving mother' in the early years of a child's development, not only for mental health but also for the child's survival. Although these studies have prompted significant changes to those procedures now used in foster homes and in the hospitalisation of children, there still remains great ignorance about infant psychology; the way children think and behave; their magic, hidden, and unique world that Saint-Exupéry intuitively perceived and labelled in "The Little Prince". It is these more subtle aspects, present in every day children and parent interaction, that this book is about.

Loneliness in children has been previously considered by several researchers, like Weiss (1973) who classified loneliness of two kinds: *social* and *emotional*. He described the 'social loneliness' as 'a perceived deficit in social integration; that is, failing to feel part of an interconnected group of friends that shares common

---

3 Bowlby was motivated in his quest by his own pre-conceptual trauma, induced by prolonged separations from his mother at a tender age.

interest and activities.' The 'emotional loneliness', on the other hand, was described as 'being the perceived lack of a truly intimate tie, the absence of a close, emotional relationship in which one feels accepted, secure, cared about, and understood'. Peplau et al (1982), from a similar perspective, stated that 'loneliness results when one experiences and recognizes a discrepancy between what one wants or hopes for in one's social relationship and what one actually achieves."[4]

The difference between this approach and the one presented in this book hinges on the particular interactions used to define loneliness, whether the emphasis is placed on the outer world or on the intrapsychic. Weiss, Peplau, and Rotenberg & Hymel (1999), for instance, based their studies on the interaction between the individual and other persons, as a kind of social consequence, or 'social-ist', if we were to use Bion terminology.[5] Whereas the kind of loneliness I am referring to now is at variance with these authors because it is 'narcissistic', meaning that it is based on the intrapsychic, between internal elements within the self, or what Klein (1963) referred to as 'internal loneliness'. In 1958, Winnicott, referring to loneliness, had expressed that the capacity to be alone was 'one of the most important signs of emotional maturity'. And also that '...after thinking in terms of three- and two-body relationships, how natural that one should go a stage further and speak of a one-body relationship". Loneliness, I believe, is present in children because they are totally dependent on their adult parents to look after them. They cannot rely on themselves, so they are always needy and usually desolated; they cannot discriminate between the intrapsychic and the external reality, lack autonomy, and *exist only in relation to the other.* Adults, on the other hand, possess

---

[4] Weiss (1973) and Peplau (1982) are both quoted by Rotenberg and Hymel (1999) pp.12 and 13, respectively.
[5] See López-Corvo 2003.

themselves, can discriminate between the intrapsychic and external reality, have autonomy and are able to rely on and *live in relation to themselves*. Children are always lonely, while adults feel alone, but not necessarily lonely, unless the child element we always have inside – which I refer to as the 'traumatised state' – has total control of our mind. These aspects are described in detail in Chapters I, V, and IX.

* * * *

When Indians from America were brought to France in the year of 1562, they were approached by Michel de Montaigne, a young magistrate and writer, who questioned them about their impression of the country. They answered in simple terms, that it was unusual that there could be men who live in abundance, while others were starving; and also that 'so many tall, bearded men, all strong and well-armed...be willing to obey a child;' (Harvey, 2008, p. 47) referring to King Charles IX, who was only twelve years old at that time. Montaigne compared this rather naïve, simple, and unpolluted form of logic from the Indians, to the avarice and religious butchery present in the European culture, like the 'massacre of St. Bartholomew', where 20,000 Protestants (Huguenots) were killed in the name of God![6] He questioned how the Indians could be considered barbarian, if '...the very words denoting lying, treason, deceit, greed, envy, slander, and forgiveness have never been heard...there is nothing barbarous or savage about them, except that we call barbarous anything that is contrary to our own habits.' They are savage, he considered, 'at the same rate that we say fruits are wild' (Ibid). Based on this conviction, Montaigne revivified the old concept of the 'noble savage', on the likelihood that the arro-

---

6 Something similar is still taking place at the present time in the acts of suicide terrorism, performed by Islamic fanatics.

gant European could have learned from the simple but natural mind of the savage.

We could apply this notion of the 'noble savage' to the naivety and simplicity that characterises all children who are born unpolluted, like a white sheet of paper with nothing written on it, and we could ponder parents to be like the Europeans, who envisage children as uneducated barbarians and usually recommend restriction, punishment and total control to 'educate them'. I do not think children are 'polymorphous perverse', as Freud once considered them to be. I prefer to think that they are 'unsaturated' and, by being thus mentally virginal, they are completely open to just about anything, even if it is perverse. In other words, Nature is mostly concerned, by means of the child,[7] with survival first; the children on the other hand, in order to survive, always use defence mechanisms based on *omnipotence* and *imitation*. These defences are the consequence of children's feelings of impotence, *loneliness*, and helplessness, and are used with the purpose of reassuring themselves, by means of magic, that they are in 'total control' and completely accepted by their powerful parents as a guarantee for endurance. Children, by being unsaturated, *are open and willing to explore just about anything* – if it does not hurt. They learn by mimicking, and at the same time lack total capacity to measure any consequence, meaning that if the parents are perverse, the children will be perverse too!

Humanity progresses for three main reasons: i) the discoveries of the secrets of life, which translate into a longer and better quality of life; ii) technology that, by shortening distances and speeding up time, produces more security and comfort; iii) women, who as

---

[7] One proof that it is Nature and not children themselves who are in charge, is the fact that *all children*, regardless of whatever culture they belong to, follow the same stages of development, like the 'refusal no' at the age of two, or 'temper tantrums' at a later age.

they become better mothers, harvest better children. To produce healthier children will require more tolerance and respect for the child, meaning that we must go down to the child's world and learn from them, instead of trying to raise them up to our own adult's level, by '*adultising*' them.

* * * * *

When I was a child and got in trouble because of some kind of naughty misbehaviour, I remember running to my grandmother's house – conveniently located next door – to find protection from my mother's rage. My grandmother, who wore long skirts as was the habit in her time, would place me under her skirt, and stand motionless while watching my mother look everywhere for me; but when my mother failed to find me, she would turn to my grandmother and attempt to lift her skirt. At that moment, my grandmother would say to my mother in a threatening manner: "don't you even think about it." Obviously, my grandmother was an important character in my life; she was my protector and rescuer. But now, already a grandfather, I do not see my grandchildren running for help either to me or to their grandmother. It seems that at the present, parents are much more tolerant than what they were in the past, no longer threatening their children with physical punishment and, as a consequence, grandparents are no longer an essential asset. However, there are other important issues still present that translate into a child's hopeless sense of loneliness, which will structure not only the pre-conceptual trauma always present in all humans, but additionally determines their own emotional profile and particular idiosyncrasy.

* * * * * *

PREFACE

When discussing children's psychopathology, professionals in the field refer to trauma as a condition that is only present in 'some children', and do not conceive the possibility of an ubiquitous condition present in all humans; possibly because they only consider what is striking and obvious and do not contemplate what Massud Khan (1963) referred to as 'cumulative trauma'. *I am completely convinced that all existing forms of psychopathology are absolutely traumatic.* The *symptoms*, meaning the way in which this 'ubiquitous trauma' – or 'pre-conceptual traumas' as I have named it – makes itself present in any human, paradoxically indicates the method by which we attempt to defend ourselves from the suffering induced by the pre-conceptual traumas. These symptoms will always depend on the culture and geography where we have been raised: the psychopathology around the equator is different from the northern territories, something I will refer to in more detail in Chapter IX.

Only two attitudes – although difficult to adopt – are required to provide a sensible upbringing of small children: '*patience*' and '*respect.*' Patience in the sense of tolerance of the child's apparent absurd behavior; and respect as a form of consideration to the child's existence as an individual. The parents must always help the child discriminate between one aspect of the child behaviour, and the child as a totality who is capable of learning from their mistakes. Serious reprimand or punishment should be mostly directed to actions performed by children that could jeopardise their health or put their life in danger. However, regardless of the reason, there should always be an attempt to help the child understand the purpose and reason for the reprimand and, if possible, to help them to participate in the final decision. Taking the child into account, meaning making them present as an active participant, will help them to become aware that they 'exist' as a human being.

A father inferred that his children, seven and four years old, had accumulated too many toys and that he and his wife were planning to sell many of them. I asked if he had discussed that decision with his children who were the 'owners' of the toys, and he said he had not because he could not be always consulting with his children on his decisions, that he had told his wife and she had agreed. In the world of the adult, when someone acts arbitrarily, there are always many facilities to use and to appeal to. However, in early childhood there are only the two parents and when they act arbitrarily there is nobody else to turn to. This stimulates the child's natural sense of helplessness to the point of absolute loneliness and total despair. Children deal with this situation with denial; they detach the emotion from the circumstance that has produced it, and then repress it. Later, when they grow older and come to deal with new traumatic situations, circumstances from the present will then unconsciously prompt the repressed emotion from the past, producing states of depression or anxiety to which we usually fail to provide a logical explanation; I have previously referred to this confusion as 'trauma entanglement'.[8]

* * * * * * * *

Most parents have great difficulty understanding their children's epistemology and struggle with achieving real communication with them, because all adults have repressed and forgotten their own childhood, of how they then felt and thought. This condition often results in the creation of two different worlds that run par-

---

8   See López-Corvo 2013, 2014.

allel, though infrequently overlap, prompting parents to resort to at least three modes of reaction: i) ignoring children, ii) trying to change them into adults, or iii) becoming impatient and often violent. From the vertex of the child, these reactions amount to feelings of unfair treatment, non-existence, but mostly, a deep sense of loneliness. Girzone (1989) referring to this matter, said the following:

> Children live in their own little world and to them it is serious business, and in their minds it all makes sense...but we can no longer enter into that world. It is lost for us forever. We were once there but somewhere along life's path have lost the key to that door that unlocks that world for us. [p. 5]

Not long ago, while I was sitting in a café, I observed a man at the next table, who was greatly focused on working on his computer. A few minutes later, a young woman, possibly his wife, came in carrying in her arms a little boy not older than three years of age, who was hugging her very tightly. After kissing him several times, she placed the boy down on the floor, then turned around, hugged and kissed the man for a few minutes, and looked at his computer screen. She turned to the boy, pulled a little car from her purse, and passed it to the child. He held it for a few seconds and then threw it angrily on the floor; she picked it up and handed it back to the boy who immediately threw it again; and then, very angrily, she scolded him for not behaving properly. The man, who remained concentrated on his work, called her; she went around the table and, amorously placing her cheek very close to his, looked at the computer screen over his shoulder. Then, the little boy approached his father and started to hit him on his leg. The father, in an angry tone, shouted: 'Stop that now! Don't do that! Behave yourself.'

Were these parents capable of understanding the meaning behind this little boy's behaviour? If the mother, for instance, had gone to another table and hugged and kissed a stranger with the same ardour she did with her husband, it is quite possible that her spouse would have become overpowered by jealousy and attacked both. Obviously, if others could have observed this scene, they might not have screamed at the husband: 'Stop that now, and behave yourself,' but rather they might have been able to understand and support the husband's rage and reaction. The only difference between the jealous child's and the jealous father's response is that any adult who had witnessed the situation would have understood and justified the parents' actions, but would have questioned the child's aggression towards his father, thinking it bad manners! However, from the child's vertex, his reaction was logical, and the emotions from the parents towards the child were absurd.

When such incomprehension by adults towards children is continuously repeated, it becomes a permanent pattern that stays within us for the rest of our life. It provides an eternal unconscious 'vitality' to the emotions present in the lonely and unfairly misunderstood child in us; after all, the etymological meaning of 'emotions' originates from 'ex' meaning 'out' and 'motion' signifying 'movement,' or, in other words, something that is so fast that it is always there ahead of us. Emotions elicited by significant facts that took place during early childhood are split and projected by the mind of the child in order to deal with the pain. These emotions remain repressed but completely detached from the particular fact that originally fashioned them; later on, however, other facts occurring during adulthood could induce what I have just referred to as 'emotional entanglement'.

* * * * * * * * *

As I have previously stated, when parents are not able to follow their children's form of thinking, they often resort either to violence or to 'adultisation' of children, or expect that the child should behave as a 'pseudo-adult' or display an 'as-if personality'.[9] As a consequence, this attitude from the parents will induce in the inchoate mind of the child, a traumatic feeling of unfairness, non-existence, impotence and a significant sense of *loneliness*. These emotions constitute the basis for a relevant aspect of what I refer to as 'pre-conceptual traumas', the early kind of trauma that is ubiquitously present in all existing individuals. 'Pre-conceptual traumas', at the same time, split everybody's mind into two different states, which I have previously named following Bion: i) a child-like part or 'traumatised state', and ii) another one capable of becoming an adult-like part that I refer to as the 'non-traumatised state'. (López-Corvo, 2014). This aspect is described in detail in Chapter I.

There is the existence of a very significant *paradox*, which always interferes with the capacity to closely follow the emotional language that structures the 'suffering side' or 'traumatised state' of any human being. This state is a direct consequence of traumatic fixations which takes place during the first years of the life of any human being, but, due to such an early start, the emotional language that assembles the 'traumatised state' follows logic based on children's thinking. The 'non-traumatised state', on the other hand, represents the normal process of physical and mental maturation as it proceeds in time from birth onwards, according to every individual's genetic endowment, influenced additionally by age, culture and experience. *The 'paradox' I have mentioned above*

---

9 The 'as if personality' represents someone who is so frightened for being excluded, that to feel loved will always please the other person's demands, to the point of becoming the 'other person's desire'. In Chapter III, I have quoted a poem from Whitman, which beautifully describes what I am trying to express now.

refers to the fact that the interaction between the 'traumatised' and 'non-traumatised,' states within any adult's mind, carries and repeats the same incomprehension that once took place between the child and their own adult parents. This means that, similar to how we as children interacted with our parents, now, when are no longer children but already adults, both states – 'traumatised' and 'non-traumatised' – inside our mind, run parallel to each other, within its own realm and inside every individual's mind, without ever touching each other. Not only are these states structured following different epistemologies, but also, and very importantly, the traumatised state is mostly unconscious while the non-traumatised is mostly conscious. In other words, the lonely outcry from a child who felt once misunderstood by his parents keeps unconsciously and eternally coming back to the same misunderstanding –although intra-psychic this time – between a child's (traumatised) and an adult's (non-traumatised) internal elements, inside the mind of every existing individual. We will return to this matter in more detail in Chapter I.

* * * * * * * * * *

In "The Little Prince", Saint-Exupery says ironically: 'Grown-ups can never understand anything on their own, and it is exhausting for children always to have to be explaining things to them...' I think however, that perhaps he was a bit too gracious in his consideration of adult behaviour, because it would be extremely difficult for a child to explain things to grown-ups because most of the time adults are too impatient, too busy or too arrogant and omnipotent, to listen and to understand children. I believe we could measure the level of cultural development in any given society, by the parent's capacity to provide their children with the same understanding, patience and respect they express to other adults they have catalogued as 'important'.

Failing to satisfy the Little Prince's demand to draw a sheep, Saint-Exupery (1943) resorted to capitalising on children's capacity to fantasise by means of 'pretending', and finally decided to draw just a plain box that 'supposedly' contained a sheep inside!

> "— That's the box. The sheep you want is inside." [Said Saint-Exupery to the Prince] "—I was very surprised." [He continued] "— To see my young judge's [the Prince] face light up. "— That's just what I wanted!" [Said the Prince] "Do you think this sheep will need a lot of grass?" [p. 8]
>
> ...My friend never explained anything. Perhaps he thought I was like him. But, personally, I'm afraid I can't see sheep inside boxes. Perhaps I'm a bit like the grown-ups. I've had to grow old. [p. 15]

The Little Prince, who represents all children, lives on a very small planet, signifying the restricted life of a child. The world of the adults is depicted by the planet of the 'King', the 'Conceited Man', the 'Drinker' and the 'Businessman'; individuals who feel so insignificant that they are continuously giving orders, demanding respect, intolerant to disobedience, having always to be in command, drunk, or too busy making money. There is a common saying in Spanish that runs as follows: 'Tell me what you pretend and I will tell you what you don't have.'

* * * * * * * * * * *

A second purpose of his book is to understand the existence of a powerful *mental* struggle between the two dialectic states: one present in the 'traumatised state' that pulls towards dependency, fear, and mental pain among other matters; and another force exercised by the 'non-traumatised state' that progressively moves towards freedom, courage, creativity, and well-being. The truth, however, is that Nature has already decided for us, denoting that, physically as well as mentally, we are forced to move from birth to death, from dependency to freedom; as if implicit in our own nature, there is a true '*drive towards freedom*'. But before I continue deliberating over these matters, I should discuss the 'theory', specifically the basic instrument on which I will be relying through this entire book in order to provide logical meaning to my elaborations; something I will attempt in Chapter I.

* * * * * * * * * * *

If we were born adults, psychopathology might not exist – except for genetic disorders – because we would have been able to defend and protect ourselves from our parents' ignorance and abusive mistreatment. However, since this is absolutely impossible, we are all doomed to endure the consequences of our unavoidable 'pre-conceptual trauma'. But we have *a second opportunity*, because, once we become adults, and are then able to use reasoning and logic – or alpha function in Bion's language – we are able to understand and provide a logical meaning to our pre-conceptual trauma and to our mental pain, which could open the doors towards a total sense of freedom and well-being.

Piaget described three main periods in the epistemological development of children. The first represents the capacity of the child to distinguish known from unknown, like how, at around eight months old, the child can recognise the face of the mother. The second period corresponds to the capacity to understand that the bad and good parents are the same, and also that the object still exists even if it is not present, an aptitude that takes place around the age of seven to eight years of age, that will help the child to deal with 'separation anxiety'. The final period is the propensity to make use of the present conditions of an object or a circumstance in order to figure out future transformations; an ability that Piaget refers to as 'formal operations' that take place around the age of twelve. At this age, the mind of the child can use simple deductive and inductive logic, very similar to how any adult might; but only with their ability to reason, because the child lacks the knowledge and skill that is acquired with time and experience.

Simple logic or common sense – alpha function, in Bion's language – could guide any individual to unravel emotional conundrums – or beta elements – resulting from pre-conceptual traumas, and to build cause-effect bridges that allow association with present mental pains; after all, only once we reach adulthood are we able to understand that we are born 'like a white sheet of paper with nothing written on it', and that *we did not deserve* whatever our parents' ignorance did to us. This insight will allow for a 'second opportunity' to find a way out from our mental suffering. *Although it might be difficult for many to imagine, I do believe – as I have just stated – that pre-conceptual traumas are the main reason for premature death!* However, the possibility of a 'second opportunity' is not a simple and easy operation that we could perform by ourselves, unless we are Sigmund Freud, the only individual capable of performing this operation by himself, since he was the creator of such methodology. At present, it will require years of personal psychoanalysis, to provide a logical sense and appropriate meaning to all emotional confusions that continuously populate our mind. Similar to a surgical intervention, psychoanalysis and psychotherapy requires someone else to perform it. *I strongly believe that the main purpose of life is 'well-being', and to truly achieve it, a proper inventiveness will be totally justified.* The question then, is how to make this procedure available to all in the future, because the domination of the mind by the child element in most humans has resulted in people who look like adults but act like children, to the point that instead of investing in life, they devote themselves to war and death. Humanity is still too primitive!

Chapter I
THE THEORY: 'PRE-CONCEPTUAL TRAUMAS'

> *The reason why we concern ourselves with things that are remembered, with our past history, is not because of what it was – although that might be quite important in its own right – but because of the mark, it has left on you or me or us now.*
> — Bion: Taming Wild Thoughts

> *For this ordered world (cosmos) is of a mixed birth: it is the offspring of a union of Necessity [traumatised state] and Intellect [non-traumatised state]. Intellect prevailing over Necessity by persuading (from Peitho, goddess of persuasion) it to direct most of the things that come to be toward what is best, and the result of this subjugation of Necessity to wise persuasion was the initial formation of the universe.*
> — Plato: The Republic

> *We suffer more often in imagination than in reality.*
> — Seneca

Introduction

In the introduction to his paper about 'a theory of thinking' (1967), Bion explained that his contribution was

> ...devised with the intention that practicing psycho-analysts should restate the hypotheses of which it is composed in terms of empirically verifiable data. (p.110)

My intention in this first chapter is to do just that with the introduction of the following argument: '*all possible forms of existing psychopathology we deal with in the consulting room are always the immediate consequence of a childhood trauma.*' I defined trauma as 'the mental condition that results when a *temporary fact* becomes *permanent* by way of repetition compulsion'. From this I have come to define two forms of traumas: the 'pre-conceptual' and the 'conceptual'. Pre-conceptual traumas are ubiquitous and represent traumas that occur early in the life of every human being, at the time when the mind is not developed enough to be capable of containing and providing the child with significant meaning. They also occur when the mother's reverie, or her intuitive capacity, fails. We could repeat here what Freud (1905) once said about the Oedipus complex; except with a little twist: '*Every new arrival on this planet is faced with the task of mastering the Oedipus complex,*' to which I add: '*that is always modified by the pre-conceptual trauma.*'

In previous publications I have described 'pre-conceptual traumas' as follows:

> *Pre-conceptual traumas, diachronically structured as a narrative of conjoined presences of absences, stand for highly toxic and emotionally organized 'parasites' that inhabit the unconscious mind from very early, feed on time and space, inhibit processes of symbolization, are projected everywhere and reproduce themselves incessantly; thereby determining not only all forms of psychopathology, but also the idiosyncrasy of every existing individual.* (López-Corvo, 2014, p. xxi)

THE THEORY: 'PRE-CONCEPTUAL TRAUMAS'

Pre-conceptual traumas represent 'constant conjunctions',[10] or facts, which, inflicted by chance, are repeated by compulsion and *will always determine the particular idiosyncrasy in all existing individuals*. 'Conceptual' traumas, on the other hand, are accidental and take place at a time when there is already a mind capable of containing them, but which fails to do so. This is due not only to the trauma's intensity, but also, and very importantly, because conceptual traumas always unconsciously trigger pre-conceptual traumas; a concept I have previously referred to as 'trauma entanglement'. (López-Corvo, 2013, 2014)

Pre-conceptual traumas split the mind in two states: the 'traumatised' and the 'non-traumatised'. The former represents the compulsive unconscious repetition of the pre-conceptual trauma, and it is structured by repressed emotions which Bion had referred to as 'beta elements'. The 'non-traumatised', on the other hand, is characterised by the natural development of mind from birth to old age, and it is ruled – according to Bion – by the 'alpha function', which can be defined as the capacity in every human being to think thoughts; or, in other words, to be able to 'mentally digest' the pre-conceptual traumas and to *contain* its painful experiences, by changing 'raw emotions' into logical and creative thoughts or "alpha elements".

---

10 A concept Bion borrowed from philosopher David Hume, to explain how an object or a fact points to another, although the ideas implicit in both are not at all related. It seems as if there is nothing logic to explain their relationship, which bears more toward a causality or cause-effect relation, where both were linked by experience, by accident, but remain associated since. Two elements are in constant conjunction, said Hume, when we infer one from the other not by reason, but from the particular experience that surrounded them, although we might fail to penetrate inside the logic of such conjunction. (López-Corvo, 2003)

The 'Traumatised' and 'Non-Traumatised' States of the Personality

Several years ago, at a conference about child analysis in Bello Horizonte, Brazil, I talked about the urgent need to establish a 'marriage' between Jean Piaget's cognitive psychology and Melanie Klein's psychology of emotions, so that both, the cognitive and the emotional sides of the mind may be integrated. It was an idea Freud was exploring in 1922 after listening to Piaget at a Psychoanalytic Congress in Berlin, when Freud became interested in Piaget's dissertation on 'symbolical thinking', because of the similarity with his own work about the unconscious (Piaget, 1961, p. 234). Anthony (1956, 1957) had also published two articles on the same subject, although more critical than integrating, referring to Piaget's work as a 'psychology without emotions'. Bion's contributions have been determinant in providing the bridge between *cognition* and *emotions*, as observed in his original work on leaderless groups. In this, Bion established the existence of two different forms of groups: the 'working' (cognitive) and the 'basic assumptions' (emotional), a consideration that served as the basis for his future paper on the 'psychotic and non-psychotic parts of the personality'. I have made use (López-Corvo, 2014) of this paper for my conception of 'pre-conceptual traumas' as well as to define two states of the mind, the 'traumatised' and the 'non-traumatised'. In relation to this matter, I have previously (Ibid) stated the following:

> In a very similar inquest, Meltzer (1978) pointed out that Bion did not discriminate between the psychotic part of personality and clinical psychoses, because of Klein's influence in considering the paranoid-schizoid position as representing the fixation point for schizophrenia. He also added that it was not clear whether Bion 'thinks that this part of the personality is

THE THEORY: 'PRE-CONCEPTUAL TRAUMAS'

ubiquitous or only present in the person who actually presents a schizophrenic disorder.' [p. 26].

Based on this statement, the experience of many other psychoanalytic researchers, as well as my own experience, I consider that Bion's reference to 'psychotic' and 'non-psychotic' is in fact a dynamic present in all human beings, resulting from early uncontained *traumatic events*. To avoid confusion – as stated by Meltzer – I decided to change Bion's term of 'psychotic and non-psychotic' to *'traumatised' and 'non-traumatised' states of the personality.*

'The traumatised state' is structured by the presence of *unconscious emotions* organised according to the specific logics of *childhood thinking*. This precise epistemology will be determined according to the time – as a point of fixation – when the particular pre-conceptual trauma was established. In other words, one can look at Piaget's cognitive work to represent not only the language of children, but also the language of all forms of psychopathology as they are present in the 'traumatised stated' of all minds. The epistemological structure of emotional thinking in adults always follows childlike logic like unconscious unremembered memories that Bion has referred to as beta elements. Or, in simple terms, the clamour of a once misunderstood child will, in the mind of an adult, eternally and unconsciously repeat itself.

This argument between cognition and emotions is not a new concern; it was already present in Plato's mind when he, by the voice of Timeous, argued that in the conception of the cosmos, there was a dialectical interaction between two opposing elements: 'Intellect' (Nous = νουσ) and 'Necessity' or 'Destiny' [Ananke = Ανανκη]. Plato stated the following: 'For this ordered world (cosmos) is of a mixed birth: it is the offspring of a union of Necessity and Intellect. Intellect prevailing over Necessity by persuading (from Peitho, goddess of persuasion) it to direct most of the things that come to be toward what is best, and the result of this subjugation of Necessity to wise persuasion was the initial formation of the universe.'[11]

There exists some resemblance between this statement made by Plato about the 'external universe' and Bion's description of the dialectic interaction between beta and alpha worlds, related to the 'internal cosmos', where the beta domain would be equivalent to 'necessity' by means of repetition compulsion, and the alpha world would correspond to the 'intellect' with the use of alpha function. An interesting variance between Plato's and Bion's positions, is found in the use of 'persuasion' by the former and 'digestion' by the latter, in order to explain how the *intellect* contains 'necessity' for Plato, and *alpha function* contains beta elements for Bion.

I have previously described 'traumas' as the result of a temporary state that changes into a permanent one, much like how the ancient footprints of dinosaurs have become eternal. Imagine a thirsty dinosaur, perhaps a tyrannosaurus, has one day walked slowly to quench its thirst to the edge of a lake that has long since disappeared, and the mud has turned to limestone. One hundred and eighty million years later heavy showers disclosed footprints engraved in the limestone revealing the footsteps of that precise morning, when the thirsty dinosaur walked to the lake. It might have been a regular uneventful act repeated by the tyrannosaurus every day, although this time, the existence of a series of *variables* conjoined to preserve the footsteps. Perhaps it was the massive weight of the animal together with specific weather conditions – like temperature, humidity, the quality of the sand, and so on – that managed to preserve the tracks forever. It meant in summary that now, when there is no longer a lake and the dinosaurs have

---

11 Translation of John M. Cooper, p. 48a.

THE THEORY: 'PRE-CONCEPTUAL TRAUMAS'

been erased from the face of the earth, its footprints produced in just one instant became preserved for eternity; or, in other words, what should have been otherwise a *temporary event* became a *permanent fact*; an *overwhelming absence* became an *everlasting presence*.

I have considered (López-Corvo, 2013, 2014) the presence of two different forms of trauma: i) One *universal*, I have referred to as *'pre-conceptual trauma'*, which is present in all existing human beings and takes place during the first years of life. ii) The other form I have referred to as *'conceptual trauma'*, which is accidental and takes place at a later age when there is a mind already, that fails to contain the facts from an overwhelming traumatic reality.[12] Due to a failure of the mechanism of 'reality testing', there is always a *continuous emotional entanglement* between *conceptual* and *pre-conceptual* traumas.

All individuals experience pre-conceptual traumas early in their life, when the 'absence" of a primary essential object – like the mother, for instance – becomes a 'permanent presence', once the rudimentary mind of the child and the mother's capacity to intuitively understand her child's distress (referred to by Bion as *reverie*) fails to contain the absence. Similar to the dinosaur's footprints, the possibility that this absence of the object changes into a lasting and chronic presence hinges on an imaginary equation, between the particular impact of the traumatic experience and the capacity of the environment to contain such a loss and turn it into a harmless and meaningless affair.

Pre-conceptual traumas are the consequence of at least three main factors: i) the discrepancy between the supremacy of the parents and the helplessness of the child; ii) the fact that parents

---

12 Most of the existing literature refers to this form of trauma as 'post-traumatic stress disorder' or PTSD.

are just ordinary people, never 'chosen by God', as children's idealisation usually leads them to believe; and iii) the *loneliness and impotence induced by the adult's incapacity to follow the logic of children, or their particular epistemological idiosyncrasies*, or in simple words: of how they think. A vignette could provide more clarity to this matter: a young woman asked about her three year old boy who started the unpleasant habit of urinating everywhere after his father had 'disappeared' when he was suddenly called away for business without giving any explanation to the child, who became very angry thinking that his father had deserted him. In these cases, a mother can determine whether the child's undesirable behaviour will disappear or become chronic. If she was to be supportive of the child's need and not to react angrily and confrontationally, the behaviour would eventually extinguish itself, but if she was to engage in a continuous struggle with the child, he might stubbornly stick to his demeanour for a very long time and even become a symptom.

It may seem reductionist to say that *all human beings have, are now, and will forever be unconsciously dealing with some form of childhood trauma, or with the clamour of the child who was once misunderstood by his parents and who is still now misunderstood intrapsychic, by the 'adult mind' or 'non-traumatised state' where 'it' now dwells*. I do believe that a simple empirical psychological observation will allow any keen eye to come to terms with this statement. Not all forms of pre-conceptual traumas are obvious and ostensible and easy to follow, as can be seen, for instance, in individuals who have been physically or sexually abused. Sometimes 'pre-conceptual traumas' can be so diluted that it becomes difficult to put it together, a concept Kahn (1963) had described as 'cumulative trauma'.

A clinical vignette could be useful: Olga was a young girl who appeared very disturbed, presenting a paranoid delusional system where she felt threatened by obscure forces that were accusing her of being a lesbian. She was the daughter of two pleasant and conscientious paediatricians and, in spite of a thorough investigation, we could not find any childhood event capable of explaining the intensity of her mental suffering, except for the fact that she was the eighth child in a family of ten children. By the time she was born, her mother was 'eight times diluted' and this 'passive absence' of a mother's necessary presence was at the core of her need and in the heart of her paranoid delusion. It was an everyday attenuated trauma, which over time had a vast and determining effect on her mind. She had projected in other women the immense need she had for her mother's presence, and confused this need with a homosexual problem, then developed as a form of defence the paranoid delusion of being accused of being a lesbian.

Most of the time pre-conceptual traumas can be understood in a few interviews, although other times it can take several weeks. In private practice it is essential to determine, as soon as possible, the specific characteristics of the particular trauma that patients have experienced in early childhood, because once you grasp the core of the pre-conceptual trauma, you will see that most of the time, what you gather from any patient's psychopathology, as well as from the transference and the counter-conference, is always a repetition of the core of the trauma. The form or how the conflict presents itself changes, but the unconscious meaning of the conflict is always the same. Some of these true traumatic characteristics can be inferred from the manner patients communicate their emotions to the therapists – something we refer to as the 'transference' – or from how the therapist responds emotionally to those feelings projected by the patient, referred to as 'counter-transference'. As stated earlier, these emotions that are always re-experienced by the adult were previously directed towards the parents during infancy, and represent traumatic conditions which have remained frozen, continuously repeating inside the unconscious mind. Gender and order of birth can also provide evidences about a particular trauma. In a family of three children, for instance, the older might feel 'abandoned', the middle one 'forgotten' and the youngest one 'abused'. But when there is only one child, pre-conceptual traumas could be structured around significant feelings of extreme sense of responsibility towards parents' well-being.

TRAUMATISED	NON-TRAUMATISED
Mental Logic:	**Mental Logic:**
Follows childlike emotional epistemology. 'Transductive' logic (from parts to parts) Structured by beta elements.	*Follows adult cognition. 'Deductive and Inductive logic'. Uses alpha function to change beta elements into alpha.*
World of Projections	**World of Reality**
(Transference-countertransference)	*(True Objects)*
Pathological Narcissism:	**Normal Narcissism:**
Time is circular: *the past being continuously repeated in the present and in the future.* Space Confusion: *No discrimination between Inner and Outer worlds.*	Time is linear. *Time and Space differentiated. Inner and Outer Worlds are discriminated.*
Loneliness:	**Aloneness:**
To exist in relation to the Other: like child to adult.	*To exist in relation to the Self: like adult to child.*
Need for an Outside 'Rescuer'	**The Only 'Rescuer' is Yourself**
Vengeful hope	**Hope by Renunciation**
Symbolisation:	**Symbolisation:**
Continuous or 'Homeomorphic'.	*Discontinuous or 'Heteromorphic'.*

THE THEORY: 'PRE-CONCEPTUAL TRAUMAS'

Another significant aspect of childhood traumas lies in how difficult it is to remember the emotional aspect of the trauma. One may be able to recall it intellectually, but the related emotions that structure the trauma usually remain repressed. Let's examine a clinical vignette: after a year into his analysis, a patient brought up a dream from which he awakes in terror feeling that he is choking because he could not swallow something. He said he remembers having this dream several times before. He does not recall any event from the previous day that could have triggered this dream, although he remembers that he was enduring dealing with a difficult and demanding problem at work. I said, 'You mean that perhaps this problem was choking you?' 'Well,' he answered, 'sometimes I feel I worry too much, that I could get fired and my family will suffer, although I know at the same time, that it would be impossible to be laid off because of something like that.' I asked if there was any situation in his childhood when he felt like choking. 'Yes,' he said, 'when I was around four or five years old, I was visiting my maternal grandmother and then swallowed several aspirins from a bottle and was brought to the hospital where my stomach was pumped; it must have been something extremely unpleasant.' I asked if his family was there, and he said that all of them were there, his mother and dad and his grandmother. The next day his grandmother had a stroke, was taken to the same hospital and eventually died. He does not remember, but this could have made him feel extremely guilty, equating the fact that she died because of what he did. Then I said: 'now we know what choked you!' Every human being shelters in their mind the existence of the traumatised eternally chiselled by the particular characteristics of their 'pre-conceptual' trauma.

There is another important aspect to consider. In psychoanalysis or psychotherapy, it is essential to the 'non-traumatised state' to make use of the coexisting alpha function present in this state to digest the beta elements that conform to the 'traumatised state' and to change them into the alpha elements required for logical thinking. A patient who I will be considering again in Chapter II starts her session with a common remark, stating – while crying – that she feels very guilty and upset because she had been having fantasies of attacking my wife. She has never met my wife, but imagined her to be ugly, angry, unpleasant and old. I said that the problem seemed not to be that she was critical, but that she was making a great deal of a fantasy – something we had discussed several times before. It seemed that an envious and angry little girl in her was attacking her mother, projected onto my wife, because she felt I was abandoning her, just as her father had done. However, since she knew all of this, I felt that the real conflict for her was that the envious and angry little girl in her had the power to control her mind, while the reasoning and logical adult in her did not make itself present and appeared helpless. I wondered if perhaps she was unconsciously testing me, by inducing me to use my own alpha function in order for her to feel that, unlike her father, I really did care for her. But if this were to be true, she was paying a high price for this with guilt and anxiety.

A woman in her forties, of Hindu extraction and who wedded in an arranged marriage when she was eighteen a man fifteen years her senior, initiated couple therapy on account of continuous pugnacious arguments between them. They unceasingly argued in a way that emulated children's 'sibling rivalry'. I said that they acted as if there were two different people: on the one hand there was an adult element (non-traumatised state) that wished to improve their relationship and had searched for therapy, and, at the same time, there was another element (traumatised state) that, similar to how they were as children, needed to accuse each other of being 'bad' in order to feel 'good' in the eyes of a mother they had inside their head, a mother they also projected onto me. There was the uncon-

THE THEORY: 'PRE-CONCEPTUAL TRAUMAS'

scious desire to make me a 'rescuer' from the helpless condition they had invented and recreated in their mind, following a script they learned when they were children. They were trapped in a cycle of repetition. However, at the end, what they really did was to forcedly place themselves into a trap. *This mechanism is always present in all couple's discrepancies and continuous mutual aggression.*

Why is that that when our child element or traumatised stated controls our mind, the non-traumatised or adult part in us does not intervene to rescue us? Why does it remain passive and rather indifferent? Bion had often remarked that projections of 'un-thought thoughts', or beta elements, always takes place together with that part of the mind capable of containing them. For instance, if someone expresses apprehension about getting inside an elevator, someone else who does not experienced that fear might explain that there is nothing to be anxious about, that an elevator is perfectly safe. This explanation, capable of containing the unreasonable dread, is missing in the phobic person and it is this form of reasoning – possibly adding unconscious meanings – that we provide in the consulting room as an interpretation. However, we could question: what makes the phobic person unable to use his or her own cogent reasoning – non-traumatised state – in order to relax the *inner* frightened little child or 'traumatised element'? We could consider three possibilities:

i) *Fear of extreme childhood aggression*; a repressed condition that can induce the disavowal of the adult part or non-traumatised state, out of fear of the child's desire to 'murder their parents', an act they were unable to perform when they were children but are capable of as adults. This aspect will be investigated in detail in Chapter X, using clinical material.

ii) *Self-envy*: a condition I have referred to previously (López-Corvo, 1992, 1995, 1997) as the attack on *logical thinking* or 'alpha function', because, for a child, 'thinking logically' belongs solely to adults or to parents as their obvious functions, as well as power and privileges. As children, we *enviously* attack this thinking capacity in our parents because we do not have it for ourselves. However, once we have grown up and become adults, we might then, by means of 'self-envy', attack the 'thinking-adult' inside of us, just as we enviously attacked our 'external parents'' capacity to think, when we were children. About this matter Bion (1962) said the following:

> The attempt to evade the experience of contact with live objects by destroying alpha-function [non-traumatised states] leaves the personality unable to have a relationship with any aspect of itself that does not resemble an automaton. Only beta-elements [traumatised state] are available for whatever activity takes the place of thinking and beta-elements are suitable for evacuation only – perhaps through the agency of projective identification. [p. 13]

And also:

> Attacks on alpha-function, stimulated by hate of envy [self-envy[13]], destroy the possibility of patient's conscious contact either with himself or another as live objects. [Ibid, p. 9]

iii) *Magical thinking*: all children use magic and omnipotent defences as a form of protection, due to the discrepancy

---

13 See: López-Corvo 1992, 1995, and 1997.

THE THEORY: 'PRE-CONCEPTUAL TRAUMAS'

between the child's helplessness and vulnerability, and the power and control exercised by the parents. It is very difficult to give up these defences that have been unconsciously used for all of one's life, as the only protection and way out. The conflict implicit in this type of childhood defence is that once we reach adulthood, obviously, childhood no longer exists, but in order to continue making use of these omnipotent defences, we have to recreate that childhood again and again inside our adult mind like a mirage, mimicking the same conditions we used to experience as a child, when we felt completely helpless in relation to our powerful parents. The whole condition becomes a *mental trap* that repeats endlessly, due to the paradox, that, in order to use omnipotent defences, the whole sense of impotence has also to be recreated, in an endless circularity, so powerful that it can completely paralyse the capacity to think logically, or to use the alpha function present in the non-traumatised state. Living in the present as adults, while at the same time our mind is continuously ruled by 'logics' fashioned by the child (traumatised state) that we used to be, without having access to our logical thinking or alpha function (non-traumatised states), will always result in the states of hopelessness, anxiety and mental suffering, which often could eventually compromise our own life.

Another aspect to contemplate is the difficulty therapists and analysts have in following the logics related to patient's psychopathology – similar to the difficulty parents have in conceptualising their children's epistemology based on the fact that usually mental suffering is a consequence to emotional confusions that were structured in childhood. This aspect will be discussed in the next chapter.

Catastrophic change as a form of defence used by the traumatised state

Bion (1965) referred to two forms of 'catastrophic change': one whose consequences involved persons outside the consulting room; the other remaining as a 'controlled breakdown' within the analytic dyad (p. 8). I believe the difference between these two forms will hinge on the seriousness of the psychopathology involved. However, I will be referring now to a third form of catastrophic change, the one taking place intra-psychically between internal part elements, such as the 'traumatised' and the 'non-traumatised' states. But before I continue this subject, I would like to summarise Bion's description of the 'catastrophic change'.

Bion borrowed René Thom's concept of 'catastrophe theory' to develop his own dissertation about catastrophic changes.[14] Following this model, we can infer that interpretation –introducing *integration* by changing *'bivalent and dialectic part-objects* into *univalent total objects*, as well as changing different kinds of *equilibration*[15] (from symmetrical to asymmetrical) – could result in a discontinuity of the mental system and sometimes in a catastrophic change. In other words, catastrophe could be induced by the introduction of *time, space,* and *symbolisation* into a currently steady or levelled state of equilibrium, which was assembled and sustained by the circular 'repetition compulsion' of childhood pre-conceptual traumas. In Chapter I, I have alluded to how pre-conceptual traumas eventually organise the existence of every human being, becoming a 'selected fact' that pro-

---

14 René Thom was a French mathematician who introduced the concept of 'Catastrophe theory'. In simple terms the theory implies that small alterations in certain factors of a nonlinear system can affect the equilibrium in such a way that it can preserve it or make it disappear, inducing significant and abrupt changes in the performance of the system.

15 See: López-Corvo 2014, Chapter XI.

gressively determines the individual's own specific idiosyncrasy. The continuous action of the interpretation (alpha function), will erode the well-structured pathology or narcissistic equilibrium, which assembles the *traumatised state of the personality*, working its way to a point where some structures might collapse, producing a 'turbulence' and giving way to a new state of equilibrium, which often results in a catastrophic change. *Discontinuation of therapy is frequently induced by uncontained catastrophic changes.*

Catastrophic change can be illustrated with numerous clinical examples. Elsewhere (López-Corvo, 2006a) I have referred to patients suffering from 'false-self" psychopathology, who felt trapped between opposite false selves: one *complying*, obvious, initially present in the transference and related to oral fixations; the other *negativistic*, hiding, initially present in the counter-transference and related to anal fixations. When the analysis progressed, and the hiding 'negativistic false self' became obvious, there was sometimes the possibility of a catastrophic change and of premature interruptions of the analysis.

For instance, a supervisee expressed her concern that her patient was 'getting worse'. The patient was a man in his fifties who displayed an excessively compliant attitude related to ambivalent feelings induced by a cruel, castrating, and punishing father. As an attempt to struggle with his repressed murderous wishes and to keep his 'murdered internal father' 'alive', he would continuously and compulsively travel to places he used to visit as a child with his father. After several interpretations attempting to link his compulsive driving to his repressed aggression, the patient portrayed a change of attitude epitomised in the session presented by the rather concerned supervisee. She started the patient's session as follows:

'I'm not doing well. I drove yesterday, and I'm still driving. Yesterday afternoon I went into the office but I didn't stay long. I seem to be on a course of disaster. I want to be on this course of disaster. There is something about it that I find appealing. I have this feeling like, yes, I want to do this. I suppose it is a form of rebellion that I couldn't act on as a child and now I can rebel. I just don't care anymore. All the normal checks and balances are thrown out the window: consciousness, work ethic . . . I just don't care anymore.'

This was a style of discourse completely different from his usual *compliant* demeanour, a drastic change towards a *negativistic* kind of false self, a form of protest that introduced the danger of a catastrophic change and the possibility of the treatment being 'thrown out of the window'. This type of 'catastrophic change' can also occur in the analysis of borderline adolescents who have been used by their families as a depository of undesired projective identifications. Once they refuse to play that role any longer, another member of the family, usually the mother, becomes symptomatic.

Homosexuality as a form of defence

David, a twenty-seven year old man, three years older than his only sister, consulted because of chronic anxiety, depression, suicide ruminations, not being very happy with his work, and feeling very ambivalent about being homosexual. He said that he studied engineering in order to please his father who was also an engineer, but now he strongly dislikes it. He described a quite difficult childhood, because of a very aggressive father and a rather passive mother. He stated that since he was a little boy his father demanded that he 'act like a man' and used to beat him often. His father accused him of being effeminate or 'too bland', and forced him to take judo classes to 'build his character'. At a given moment, he expressed that he suspected I was trying to make him 'straight'. I said that 'there seems to be in him a powerful need to "invent" other persons like his own father, by means of projective and introjective identifications', as if he felt he could only exist in relation to others, and not to himself. I also added that I was not interested in his sexuality, but in the fact that he seemed not to be aware that he was already a man, that he was autonomous, on his own, and existed just by himself alone, on his own accord and was no longer a little boy. Since he continued claiming that I wanted to change his sexuality, I felt that he was insisting because a part of him strongly needed this transference, making me his 'accusing father'. I started to wonder about what was the true meaning behind this powerful 'need', and considered several possibilities: i) he experienced a great dialectical ambivalence between killing his father by disregarding or ignoring him, while at the same time, bringing him back to life by acknowledging and pleasing him, as shown by his becoming an engineer like his father; ii) as a child, he became aware that his father was intensely homophobic, and, as a form of revenge and controlling, he became homosexual; now however, as an adult, he was unsure that he wanted to be homosexual, but since this was his best 'weapon' to attack and control his father, he was afraid to give it up, because he then would be completely defenceless and vulnerable; iii) his mind was controlled by the child in him, who felt lost and very lonely and in need of his father to rescue him, even if by doing so he feared him too; however, through the years, he had become so accustomed to this condition, that, even if he felt threatened by his father's anger, he preferred this to being lonely. At the end, I said to him, 'it all depends on which mental part of him controlled his mind, whether it's the "helpless child" he used to be, or the "powerful and thinking adult" that he was now'.

At a given moment, he described a dream that woke him up in the middle of the night, and portrayed his anger towards his parents as well as his own guilt and ambivalence. *'I was speaking to my mother who had decided to donate her organs and that I was supposed to do the operation, which would kill her, and she was ready to die. I tried to convince her otherwise, but she was certain. Next, I was speaking to my father, who also wanted to donate his organs and die. Two strange men came into the room and began to approach me and beat me violently, and killed me, then I woke up.'*

A second opportunity

We are a product of Nature, usually born pure from influences, with the exception of genetic pathology. Afterwards, we will be always marked by the ignorance and hegemony of our ordinary parents, who will at all times induce a ubiquitous traumatic condition that I have already referred to as 'pre-conceptual trauma'. This traumatic situation is mostly the outcome of a fatal combination between the helplessness of the child and the supremacy of the adult parents. This sense of helplessness will always trigger in the child a magic and omnipotent defence with the purpose of 'neutralising' the powerful control exercised by the parents.[16] At the same time, 'emotional confusions and infantile logics' – I refer to as the 'traumatised state' – repeat themselves in a circular and endless fashion. As our mind matures as we grow and become independent adults, we evolve to the 'non-traumatised state', with possibly even more intellectual capacity than our parents had. After all, one of the reasons humanity has progressed is because children, most of the time, have been much more creative than their parents. I have already specified that there is always a continuous dialectic interaction between the 'traumatised' and the

---

16 I will come back in more detail to this form of defence in the next chapter.

THE THEORY: 'PRE-CONCEPTUAL TRAUMAS'

'non-traumatised' states, and our regular way of dealing with reality will constantly depend on which one of these states controls our mind. Using our 'alpha function' – following Bion's theory on thinking – present in the 'non-traumatised state' or, in simple terms, using our capacity to think logically, we might be able to contain our childhood's traumatised elements and provide for ourselves a *second possibility* of freedom from the detrimental effects induced by the 'traumatised state'. After all, this possibility is what psychoanalysis attempts to achieve with the use of the analyst's own alpha function. As powerful[17] adults, we are granted a "*second opportunity,*" by understanding the reasons behind our 'pre-conceptual trauma,' and by finding ways to provide logical meaning to the mental pain that results from what I consider a "mental trap," a mechanism that will be explored in Chapter IV.

The capacity to achieve this 'second opportunity' is not a simple task, since we have to deal with two imperatives: in the first place, the immense resistance to give up the *omnipotent* and *magic* defences, we have created using our early childhood logics, and to which we have become quite accustomed, after unconsciously 'relying' on these defences for most of our life. The second quandary relates to the inordinate difficulty of attaining a clear look and understanding of something that remains so close to our self, that it is very difficult to see; something that harkens back to what Shakespeare once said: "...for the eye sees not itself." This is why, in order to find a solution to these ongoing troubles, it will be absolutely indispensable to find outside help, either from a psychoanalyst or from a psychoanalytic psychotherapist[18].

---

17 I mean 'powerful' in comparison to the 'helplessness' of the child.
18 "The Greeks had already referred to this: (*Ancient Greek:* φοῖνιξ, *phoînix*) is a long-lived bird that cyclically regenerates or is otherwise born again. Associated with the sun, a phoenix obtains new life by arising from the ashes of its predecessor. According to some sources, the phoenix dies in a show of flames and combustion, although

The main purpose of this second opportunity would be, to attempt to regress to the time when we were born, when we were untouched and not and yet marked by destiny, by the hands of our ignorant and 'dangerous' parents; but also, and very importantly, to *forgive* them and to *forgive* ourselves, for our mistakes and for what we all have done wrong. The main issue will be to conceive the possibility of 'containing' the repetitious trauma in our mind, instead of being 'contained' by it and to act it out. In other words, in order to become who we really are, we have to acknowledge that whatever marks were inflicted in our soul, *we did not deserved them! We must become our best unconditional loving friend, one who will create and maintain, an inner state of wellbeing!*

---

there are other sources that claim that the legendary bird dies and simply decomposes before being born again.[1] There are different traditions concerning the lifespan of the phoenix, but by most accounts the phoenix lived for 500 years before rebirth. Herodotus, Lucan, Pliny the Elder, Pope Clement I, Lactantius, Ovid, and Isidore of Seville are among those who have contributed to the retelling and transmission of the phoenix motif." (Quoted from Wikipedia)

Chapter II
THE 'TRAUMATISED STATE' IS STRUCTURED FOLLOWING THE LOGIC OF CHILDREN'S THINKING

In 1959, Klein published a paper entitled '*Our Adult World and its Roots on Infancy*' where she investigates 'the behavior of people in their social surroundings', how 'the individual develops from infancy to maturity', and concludes that 'An exploration of the individual's development takes the psycho-analyst back, by gradual stages, to infancy." Bion (1967), on the other hand, has established a difference between the child's mind, or 'rudimentary infant consciousness', which lacks the presence of an 'alpha function', and the adult's mind which is capable of producing creative thoughts. He also described four aspects used to define the mental structure of this rudimentary psyche: i) thinking, associated with modification or evasion; ii) projective identification, associated with evasion through evacuation, which should not be confused with ordinary projective identification; iii) omniscience; iv) communication. (p. 117).

There are several child-like 'emotional performances' often observed in the 'traumatised state' of adult patients, and I would like to consider some of them:

i) *The trail of envy;*
ii) *Black and white or zero-sum form of thinking;*

iii) *Impotence vs. omnipotence;*
iv) *Confusion between the whole and the parts;*
v) *Confusion of time: past, present and future;*
vi) *Lack of discrimination between projection and reality or failure to discriminate between external and internal realities;*
vii) *'Egocentrism' or self-centred behaviour, paranoia and tendency to exist in relation to others and not to the 'Self';*
viii) *Fear of dependency;*
ix) *Sense of being unborn or not existing;*
x) *Generalisation.*
xi) *Not trusting their judgement and unable to question the nature of their symptoms.*

By using clinical examples I will now consider each of these emotional confusions as they are present in children:

i) The trail of envy:

This mechanism is discussed in detail in Chapter VIII. However, I will summarise now what I refer to as 'the trail of envy'. Children instinctively experience a 'nameless fear' about the possibility of being abandoned, a fear that will not only induce a need to please their parents' demands, but also to reach a 'state of total perfection' in order to feel loved, At the same time they project in others (mostly their siblings) anything they consider 'bad'. Also, these feelings can be projected too, splitting the object into 'bad persecutor' and 'good idealised,' the latter sensed as a possible 'rescuer'. In this condition, children compete with each other and become very envious of whatever they idealise and project, something that very often could induce acting out. I recall a video in which a child, around eight or nine years of age, is sitting in the front seat of their car next to his mother who is driving. He is singing beautifully and with great dexterity, to his mother's delight, while a younger child sitting in the back of the car is desperately screaming at the top of his lungs. In summary, the usual trail of envy follows the following stages: a) introjection of the bad and self-debasing object, b) projection of the idealised object, and c) envy towards idealised object projected. However, this interaction is usually introjected, and what was once envied in the outside object, is, with time, envied intra-psychically between internal part self-objects as a form of 'self-envy'.[19]

ii) Black and white or zero-sum form of thinking:

There is the impression that certain individuals unconsciously abide by the existence of some kind of a model of absolute perfection, against which they continuously compare themselves, as a result of a very sadistic and demanding super-ego. It is either absolutely perfect or no good at all, an impasse without any other possibility, which will always result in a total failure because 'nobody is born learned' and we all learn from mistakes, from experience. Associated with this emotional confusion is also a tendency to reject any interpretation that might be experienced as a form of criticism; in this quandary the only solution I have found is to resort to 'intrapsychic interpretations', a mechanism I have already described in detail previously (López-Corvo, 1999, 2006a). There I considered the existence of three possible forms of interpretation: *extra-transferencial*, *transferencial*, and *intrapsychic*. In reality, every mental conflict is originally intrapsychic, but will become external by means of projective identifications directed to the analyst as well as outside the consulting room. By focusing on the intrapsychic, we will be dealing with the true source of the conflict, instead of concentrating on its projection in the external objects; a strategy that could be useful when we are

---

19 See Chapter X.

dealing with a very demanding superego, like masochism, paranoia, and so on.

iii) Impotence vs. Omnipotence:

Omnipotence is the main defence children always use in order to deal with their intuitively sensed biological helplessness,[20] and with their feeling of complete *loneliness*. Imagine for instance, two adults conversing in a closed room while a toddler walks around under their surveillance. Suddenly, the child discovers the electric plug on the wall and tries to investigate it. In the face of the danger, the adults jump up and remove the child from the plug while telling him not to touch it again because it is dangerous. Once the child is let free, he will immediately run to the wall again, touch the plug and turn to look at the adults with a smile and a twinkle in his eyes. Is the child interested in investigating the plug? No. He has discovered with immense delight a magic button that makes him feel powerful, because whenever he touches it, the *important adults jump!* Omnipotence as a defence to compensate for feelings of impotent *loneliness* and fear of dependency, are usually associated with impatience, anger and exaggerated need to control, like for instance 'the omnipotence of words' seen in swearing. I remember several years ago, when my neighbour's four year old little boy was climbing the fence between the two houses. I approached him and said he shouldn't do that, it was dangerous and he could fall and hurt himself. Since he continued doing it, I came closer and insisted that he should stop or I was going to call his father. He then came down, moved to the middle of his backyard and from there started to scream angrily at me: 'poo, pee,

---

20 Superheroes represent the creativity of the helpless 'child' present in the traumatised state, that resorts to idealisation and magic means, in order to compensate as well as being 'rescued'. It is something present in all idealised superheroes like, Superman, Batman, Spiderman, and so on.

shiet, I hate you.' It was his powerful repertoire, an arsenal of 'dangerous words' aimed at destroying me completely! This is a mechanism very often present in adults, who even can literally kill as a response to feeling insulted when any of these words are uttered at them. This is also commonly present in religions that are sensitive to notions of blasphemy.

iv) Confusion between the whole and the parts:

This aspect is usually a consequence of the parents' incapacity to discriminate between the child as a whole and a specific behaviour they try to change or reprimand; after all, you are not correcting the child as a human being, but trying only to modify a specific and unacceptable action. Punishment should never be imposed on a child in an authoritarian way, without taking into account the existence of the child as an individual who should participate and comprehend the reason that motivated the punishment. To do otherwise carries the danger of the child not being aware that he/she exists as a whole, as an individual. In any case, parents should try to reprimand mostly when dealing with a situation that could be dangerous to the child's health or integrity.

A clinical example: Armand, a middle child with an older brother and a younger sister, was working as a manager. He was asked by his boss to address Mrs. L, an employee who was considered not to be performing at her best. Mrs. L later complained to Mr. D., Armand's boss, that he was too rough and aggressive when he talked to her, a situation that prompted Mr. D to address Armand about this behaviour and to tell him that perhaps he was too direct in his approach. After explaining this situation to me in our session, Armand said that he had had a troubled weekend, because he felt very upset about the whole state of affairs. I said that I couldn't see what made him so upset; after all, they were only complaining about his approach or the style he used to address the matter to

Mrs. L; he could either question the assessment if he disagreed with it, or acknowledge if he felt that what Mr. D said to him was valid; he could have learned from the experience and perhaps even changed his approach. Perhaps he was also too hard on himself, punishing himself to the point that he was confusing the whole with the parts. He felt that a simple mistake was enough to make him entirely no good at all, like throwing away your car because you have a flat tire. He said what upset him most was that he was feeling very guilty, because when he arrived home that evening his four year old daughter was bitterly crying. He lost his temper and shouted at the child, and his wife appeared and held the little girl trying to console her. A few minutes passed and the girl continued crying and then he turned to his wife and screamed angrily that what she was doing wasn't working.

After a pause, he remembered a dream: *he was watching the fire of a chimney that reminded him of the one he had in his house in his original country where he grew up. Then suddenly he saw a puppy, a little dog trying to get out from the fire of what appeared to be like a long tunnel. He then opened the door of the chimney and pulled the puppy out and saw that his paws were burned.* I said that it seemed that a little child in him, like the puppy, finds himself in a fire of his own creation, from where he is rescued by an adult part of himself, but not without getting burned. The question at the end is how could the adult in him have prevented that inner child element (traumatised state) from taking over his mind, and inducing him to confuse the whole with the parts? By being unable to learn from mistakes – or experience – and, sparked by his sense of loneliness, feelings of jealousy were induced in him at the sight of his 'wife-mother' consoling his 'daughter-sister'. And most important of all, he needed to be able to avoid that a 'pleasant weekend' could have changed into a 'terrible fire'! The solution would hinge on the ability of the adult, or non-traumatised part of him, to take over his mind and to rule it in a logical manner, instead of his mind being contained by the confused child element within.

v) Confusion of time: past, present and future:

Time confusion between the past and the present represents the physiology of transference as well as 'repetition compulsion', a subject I will be deliberating in detail in the next chapter. The confusion between present and future is a form of defence related to Freud's 'signal theory', a concept he introduced in his 1926 article: *'Inhibition, Symptom, and Anxiety'*. It is a type of defence used by the ego, to deal with the concern related to a given future event, which is anticipated as very traumatic. In order to deal with the anxiety induced by the expectation, the event is continuously reproduced as a phantasy – or signal – before it takes place. The individuals might not have clear insight into the true traumatic intensity of the 'real event', but instead of remaining ignorant about and trusting their capacity to eventually deal with it, they react to the phantasy as if it were the real event, increasing the level of anxiety ahead of time. It is a situation related to lack of self-confidence, as we might see in children who do not trust their own judgement. For instance, were we to ask any ten year old child to stay by themselves in the downtown of a city, they would refuse and could feel anxious about the prospect of staying there alone even if they knew their home address and telephone number. A clinical vignette might be helpful: a patient is rather anxious, as he has being waiting for a clinical evaluation from his doctor about some chest pain he was experiencing. Two days before the assessment he had the following dream: *He was parking his car in a parking lot, but forgot to put on the hand brake and just as he was coming out, the car moved ahead and hit a truck that was in front, and this car also moved and hit the next car. He felt very worried in the dream, about what the drivers were going to say to him, and about the amount of money, he might have to pay for the damage. Then the owner of the car who was a nice looking woman, went to her car, and he approached her to explain what happened, but instead of being angry, she was very nice and even seductive towards him, and told him not to worry. Then came the truck's owner, and he then felt that for sure, he was going to be very upset, but after he told him about the accident, the man smiled and said 'It's okay. It's just an old truck.'*

vi) Lack of discrimination between projection and reality, or failure to discriminate between external and internal realities:

This confusion represents the difficulty in differentiating between the 'other' and the 'self' as diverse entities. The individual fails to understand that whatever the 'other' does – whether thought, word or deed – may have nothing at all to do with them, that it could have been just the other's way, and that he was like that even before they met him. Often this manifests as the type of confusion we see in paranoia, in which nothing is accidental. Every experience and everything that happens around this person is directly related to their ego. It is always purposely determined.

A clinical example might be of help: a forty-three year old woman of Latin extraction, the middle child of three siblings, bitterly complained about her husband's decision to buy a new car for his mother at a time when she had asked him to buy a car for her. I asked her why it was so upsetting that her that her husband had decided to buy a car for his mother? She answered that she felt as if he loved his mother more than he loved her. I wondered what could have induced her to make her mother-in-law's issues her own issue; that perhaps her mind at that moment was controlled by a confused child element in her, that confused her husband with her father or her younger brother, and her mother-in-law with her own mother, because it was obvious that her mother-in-law could not compete with her. After all, she was married to her son, living with him, having babies with him and so on. The other possibility was the remnants of an old resentment against her father who she felt had preferred her older sister, or perhaps against her own mother who 'provided' a penis to her younger brother – which she confused with the car – and failed to 'provide' one to her. She said she would have to think about that. From the perspective of the emotional and confused little girl in her, if her mother-in-law got a car from her husband at the same time she did, both of them would be the same; there would be no differentiation between them, as if her own identity as an individual, or what in fact she really is, comes from outside, from the other and not from her; it was defined in relation to the other. 'Truth,' – as Bion has often said – 'does not need a thinker;' meaning that this person has to become whatever she already *is*, whatever that might be, and not what others might decide she is. She should exist only in relation to herself, and not in relation to others.

One day I visited my daughter's house and found my three and half year old grandson naked in the living room and pulling his penis. I said: *'Oh, so you have a penis.'* He nodded his head affirmatively. *'Are you the only one who has a penis in this house?'* He said *'no.' 'What about your father?'* I asked, and he said: *'Yes.' 'And your mother?' 'No,'* he answered. *'And your sister?' 'No.' 'And do I have a penis?' 'No,'* he said. He had never seen me naked, so his conclusion was based on empirical observation only, as if he was not able to generalise and to conceive that the presence or absence of a penis was based on gender and not the other way around, as a random distribution of a particular quality that some will have and others not.

vii) 'Egocentrism' or self-centred behaviour, paranoia and tendency to exist only in relation to others and not to the 'Self':

In ancient times, Aristarchus of Samos introduced the 'heliocentric theory, according to which, unlike what is observed by the naked eye, the earth moves around the sun and not the opposite. This theory disappeared for two thousand years until Copernicus proved it again, putting him at odds with the church-sanctioned dominion of the 'geocentric theory' that had dominated since the time of Aristotle. Heliocentric and geocentric are two oppositional theories; the first one is true but not obvious, and the second one is obvious but not true. There are still remnants from the geocentric theory; for instance, when we say: 'I will see you tomorrow at sunrise.' Obviously, the sun does not rise, it is the earth that moves around it (Bion, 1992, pp. 154–156). Similarly, in the analytic situation, a patient may defend their own personal 'geocentric theory' – a scientific deductive system he has used all his life, based on what appears to be obvious but is not true. The analyst, on the other hand, uses a different deductive system – one that is similar to the heliocentric theory is based on the truth but may not be obvious. It is their job to convince the patient of its effectiveness to reduce mental pain.

For example, a patient with an important false self-pathology said very apologetically after lying down: 'Yesterday when I was going to sign the document to buy the new apartment I was very anxious. Imagine of being afraid about such a foolish thing…I thought I was doing better, but I can see that I am still failing.' According to her 'geocentric' position, she presupposes 'in the transference' the existence of an idealised model that demands from her a complete absence of anxiety as a true 'instrument for achievement' – like passing a test; or the contrary, suffering from anxiety would mean a total failure. In the transference, this represents that she thinks the analyst is also expecting her not to feel anxious, and will view her feeling anxious as a fiasco. Instead of the analyst going around her (heliocentric), she goes around the analyst (geocentric). Bion believed that an attempt to introduce a different scientific deductive system with the use of the interpretation would induce mental turbulence.

While training as a child analyst I was asked by the head of the department to talk to a four or five year old little girl whose parents had died in a terrible traffic accident. I recall asking this beautiful quite manic froglike jumping little girl if she knew where her parents were. She pointed to the ceiling and answered sadly: 'They are up in the sky.' When I asked, 'Why did they go there?' she replied: 'Because I peed on my bed.' All children feel they are the centre of the universe and believe that whatever takes place around them is always directly related to themselves; it is a defence children use in order to compensate for their feeling of powerlessness, 'insignificance' and mostly loneliness. They are ruled by 'primary narcissism' and projective and introjective identifications, meaning that they are unable to discriminate between their own mind and the world outside of them. Child thinking is egocentric and reveals only what the child is thinking at that particular moment, heedless of whether what he/she is discerning makes sense to anybody. When children express something, they are unmindful of whoever is listening to them. It is this egocentrism that is at the centre of paranoia, when adults, for instance, take the issues of another person and make them their own.

viii) **Fear of dependency:**

Fear of dependency is a common feeling related to 'trust' and fear of being hurt. In some cases, it can reach extremes, usually when pre-conceptual traumas have been too intense. In these patients, signs of alexitimia become present, as a defence from the terror of being physically injured. I observed these signs in a woman who had a surgical intervention to correct a 'spina bifida occulta' when she was six years old; also in a patient born with a dislocated shoulder (more on him in Chapter XI). 'Fear of dependency' could also be observed in the ethos of some Asian, European and North American countries, where 'emotional needs' are regarded as shameful and a sign of weakness of character. However, this fear is always absent in most of the Mediterranean population, where dependency is openly expressed and alexitimia seldom observed, making you wonder if these emotions are in some ways weather-related. Feelings of need and dependency are normally present in all children; but perhaps in climates where the weather is life threatening, with intense and prolonged winters and where help is scarce and expensive, the everyday preparation of getting dressed and ready to properly face the inclemency of the weather is very challenging to parents. Short of time because they usually work, mothers may be more demanding that their children become independent very early, usually by pointing to 'dependency' as an expression of 'shameful weakness'. Contingent on the pre-conceptual trauma, 'dependency' would often be repressed and continuously projected on the other by means of projective identifications. In therapy, for instance, this can often be observed in patients who reject treatment, or while in therapy take holidays ahead of the analyst, or delay payment. 'Dependency' may also be gender related, more difficult for men than for women to express. As a result, women are more inclined to search for emotional help than men.

ix) Sense of being unborn or not existing:

Osho once stated that the main concern for humans was not so much to wonder if there is life after death, but to know if there is life before death! Bion had used the notion of 'animate' and 'inanimate'

THE 'TRAUMATISED STATE'

to distinguish between the feeling of being 'human' and of 'material objects' respectively. He stated that babies who have been subjected to external aggression will attack the breast by obstructing love coming from the breast. As a consequence, they fear retaliation from the breast; however, in order not to die from starvation – if they were to discard sucking completely – the baby splits the breast[21] into *good*, or material for survival, and *bad*, relating to love and affection. About this Bion (1962) said:

> This makes breast and infant appear inanimate with consequent guiltiness, fear of suicide and fear of murder [it is easier to destroy something inanimate than something alive]...The need for love, understanding and mental development is now deflected, since it cannot be satisfied, into the search for material comforts [p. 11]

There is also an important aspect related to the parent's narcissistic structure, which induces them to sense and treat their small children as if they were just an extension of themselves, instead of regarding them as distinct human beings who deserve consideration and respect. A relevant aspect related to this matter, for instance, is how parents usually punish their children, when feeling troubled by the children's normal, although erratic and unpredictable, behaviour. Penalisation should be mostly oriented at protecting children from endangering their life and well-being. *Punishment should always be exacted with the child's participation and agreement. It should never be imposed vertically and angrily, without consulting and discussing the punishment with the child in question.*

---

21 Bion referred to this kind of split as 'enforced splitting'. For more detail see López-Corvo, (2003)

x) Generalisation:

Piaget (1961) described the following observation about one of his children, age two years, ten months and eight days:

> *J. had a temperature and wanted oranges. It was too early in the season for oranges to be in the shops and we tried to explain to her that they were not yet ripe. 'They're still green. We can't eat them. They haven't yet got their lovely yellow colour.' J. seems to accept this, but a moment later, as she was drinking her camomile tea, she said: 'Camomile isn't green it's yellow already...Give me some oranges!' The reason here is clear: if the camomile is already yellow, the oranges can also be yellow – a case of 'active' analogy or symbolic participation. [316]*

Conceptualisation is not established in children, on the identity of the object as a whole, but on a particular quality that could determine that two different objects are the same if they were to share a common quality, like the colour yellow in the camomile and the oranges. It is a kind of symbolical confusion present in children, as well as in the 'traumatised state' of any adult. I have previously described (Lopez-Corvo, 2014) two forms of symbolisation: i) *homeomorphic* and ii) *heteromorphic*, based on two important qualities of the internal objects: the *form* and the *meaning*. In the *homeomorphic symbolisation* the object changes form; the breast, for instance, progresses through a successive series of transitional objects, such as the pacifier, the thumb, security blanket, masturbation, cigarettes, alcohol, and so on. All look different, but the unconscious *meaning* will be always the same in each of these transformations. Using Freud's expression we could say that a 'cigar is not always a cigar'. This form of symbolisation is constantly present in the thinking of children and in the traumatised state, giving rise to 'generalisation'. We often see this in the transference, when the analyst is confused with the patient's parents. *'Heteromorphic symbolisation',* on the other hand, is present in the non-traumatised state and is structured as the opposite of the homeomorphic type, where the *form* could be similar but the *meaning* is different. We see this, for instance, in the oedipal resolution, when an individual finds a spouse who looks physically similar to one of their parents, but is a totally different person; or again in Freud's apocryphal expression, 'sometimes a cigar is just a cigar'.

Charles, a thirty-five year old single man, consulted because of chronic anxiety and bouts of depression. He was the middle and only boy of three siblings, four years younger than his older sister, and three years older that the younger one. Being a boy, his birth was much celebrated, until the birth of his younger sister and the diminishing presence of his mother due to postpartum depression. At the present he has a steady girlfriend, but, since he has to travel often, he likewise has other girlfriends in different places; he also said that he would never marry or have children because he does not trust women because he thinks that all women can be unfaithful, and eventually will hurt him, just as his mother did to him by preferring his father and siblings. I said to him that being a boy, born four years after his older sister, and then losing his mother due to the birth of his younger sister and her postpartum depression, introduced in him such ambivalent contrast between 'having all and having nothing' has controlled him his whole life. *All women have become his own mother*, because, at the same time that he was possessed by the need to find a woman who could love him unconditionally in spite of him being unfaithful, he also projected on them his resentment towards his own mother and exercised revenge on women by rejecting fidelity and marriage.

xi) **Not trusting their judgement and unable to question the nature of their symptoms:**

If we were to leave a nine year old child alone in downtown, far from his house, he would feel extremely apprehensive. He might be a bright child who knows his home phone and address, but he does not trust anybody, because he lacks good judgement and experience; mostly he does not trust himself and lacks self-confidence. Bion (1967) had referred to the 'rudimentary conscious or mental apparatus' to describe the undeveloped mind of the child, which I think is also part of the logic present in the 'traumatised state' within the mind of any adult individual. Such rudimentary mental apparatus is not capable of changing sense-data into alpha elements, and will need to 'evacuate these elements into the mother, or any other adult, relying on her to do whatever has to be done to convert them into a form of suitable for employment as alpha elements by the infant'. (Ibid, p. 116) In relation to this aspect, I have previously stated the following:

> A rudimentary conscious cannot deal with those tasks that would ordinarily be considered as affairs suitable for an adult's mind [non-traumatised state] that can contain them. When the relationship between this primitive mind and maternal reverie is broken, such rudimentary conscious cannot deal with the burden that it must now support, giving then place to the establishment of an internal object ('projective-identification-rejecting-object means'), which instead of providing the infant with an understanding, such object, provides a willfully misunderstanding with which the infant is now identified. [Lopez-Corvo, 2003]

When the 'traumatised state' is in control of the 'non-traumatised', these logics predominate in the mind.

THE 'TRAUMATISED STATE'

A clinical case could be of some help. Gustav, a patient I will be discussing in Chapter XII, was born with a dislocated shoulder that marked him for life. We considered as a hypothesis that perhaps when he was a baby alone in his crib, and crying for his mother, she responded by picking him up, but the excruciating pain in his shoulder would set him off screaming. His mother, not able to understand why his reaction was so unusual and so different from his older brother's, may have left him again alone in his crib. He felt hurt physically and mentally, the former because of a horrible pain in his shoulder, and the latter for being rejected and abandoned for hours alone in his crib. Now, after thirty years, he is still terrified of being so hurt, and to protect himself he tries to avoid any form of emotional closeness, as if he recreates again and again the same tragedy he once experienced in his crib. Even though the adult or 'non-traumatised state' in him knew that such a condition no longer existed, he continued reacting in the same manner as he did in the past, when he had a dislocated shoulder and was completely helpless and unable to protect himself.

When insisting with the interpretation about this matter, he recalled a dream: *was invited by someone to board a boat and as they continued into the open sea, there were many dolphins swimming around the boat that were trying to jump inside the boat to attack him, possibly to cut his head off.* He offered no associations and I pointed out that there was a discrepancy in the dream, because, as he elaborated his dream, he had chosen the wrong fish, because dolphins are extremely gentle and, as far as I know, have never attacked a human; if there were sharks, for instance, the situation might have been quite different. I thought his dream meant that there were no external reasons for him to feel afraid of getting emotionally close to anybody, and that his fear was completely invented by him. The purpose of his unconscious using this dream was to provide him with a message: fearing that gentle dolphins will cut off his head is the same as fearing emotional closeness will result in him getting hurt.

How Children Protest

Most of the time the communication between parents and small children is similar to the interaction between persons who speak a different language, not so much from the side of the children, who always behave and act according to their own biological nature, but from the parents, who, out of ignorance, are unable to follow children's language, or to understand how they think, communicate and express themselves. I believe the ways in which parents misunderstand their child's epistemology is one of the important themes in Antione de Saint-Exupery' book, *The Little Prince.*

Usually parents believe they are communicating with their children; however, most of the time they are interacting with their own narcissistic structure projected on the child like a mirror. In other words, they are not really interrelating with the child but only with themselves! All children intuitively dispute this form of abuse, of being completely bypassed and ignored; I think that it would be more accurate to say that it is Nature that protests through the children, because at that age, regardless of their culture, colour, or geography, when the rudimentary mind lacks the capacity to grasp what exactly is taking place, all children around the world will protest using *temper tantrums* and the '*refusal no*'. The '*refusal no*' is present between two and three years of age, and '*temper tantrums*' at a later age.[22] The 'refusal no' can also be observed in two other conditions: in very old people and in catatonic schizophrenia. The three states: small children, seniors and catatonics, have one thing in common: a

---

[22] I say 'at a later age' because temper tantrums can often be observed at all ages!

sense of 'non-existence'. The children have this sense because they are too little to have advanced much in their life and to acquire a true sense of existence; the elders are at the other extreme, being close to disappearance by death; and the psychotics because the essence of this pathology consists in omnipotent defences in compensation for immense feelings of non-existence. I remember a young catatonic patient in a mental hospital who used to stand in the garden for hours, motionless like a statue, with his right hand raised to the level of his waist holding together the index finger and the thumb. His deep sense of 'insignificance' – of not existing – was so deep that he compensated by believing that by holding his fingers together he could make everything around him happen: the wind to blow, the sun to move, the clouds to pass, and so on. He compensated for his own feelings of total helplessness by becoming like Atlas: completely responsible for holding together the whole universe. He was truly terrified that, if he was to open his hand completely, the whole world would collapse, and so he did not move!

At a given moment during the psychotherapy of a young mother, she mentioned that she was planning to have her three-year-old and only son's tonsils removed the following week. When I asked what determined such an action, she produced her child's picture on her cell phone to show me that he had 'circles around his eyes' and stated that she and his doctor were convinced it was a consequence of his 'infected tonsils'. As I tried to convince her to wait and to take some time to discuss the matter, I started to feel very anxious and helpless, and I thought that I was either connecting my own helplessness in relation to my patient's strong stubbornness, or I was connecting countertransferentially to my own childhood helplessness. I then said to her that an intervention of such magnitude in such a young child was going to produce devastating consequences because in his mind he was going to feel extremely helpless and lonely. He would be unable to understand what was going on, and could eventually feel extremely frightened and guilty, thinking that he was being punished for something terrible he had done. She stubbornly insisted that she had thought about it and felt that it was the best for her child. This patient was the youngest of five girls, who as a child felt rather abused by her older sisters as well as her parents. At a given moment I said to her that perhaps she was the last opportunity for her parents to have a boy, and, by being a girl, she was a source of disappointment to them. She reflected for a moment and said she had never thought that before. I felt that possibly she was very envious of her son, as, if she had been a boy like him, her life would have been quite different because she would have been much indulged. Perhaps her apparent 'castrating aggression' towards her son was the consequence of a little girl's envy towards him, for being a boy.

Chapter III
HOW CHILDREN THINK

> There was a child went forth every day;
> And the first object he looked upon, that object he became;
> And that object became part of him for the day,
> Or a certain part of the day, or for
> Many years, or stretching cycles of years
>
> — Walt Whitman
> Leaves of Grass

Introduction

In 1959, in her book "Envy and Gratitude", Klein reaffirmed Freud's early statements about how the transference re enacts in the psycho-analyst's 'very early situations and emotions':

> Therefore the relationship to the psycho-analyst at times bears, even in adults, very childlike features, such as over-dependence and the need to be guided, together with quite irrational distrust...mental life is *influenced*[23] by earliest emotions and unconscious phantasies. [pp. 247, 248]

However, I do prefer to say that mental life, more than '*influenced* by earliest emotions', is in reality 'determined,' at least in relation to an important aspect of the mind which I have referred to as the 'traumatised state'.

---

23 My italic.

What makes the 'emotional language' present in the 'traumatised state' of any adult structure follow logic based on a child's form of thinking? It seems as if there is an emotional child in every human, hidden under the physical appearance of a grown-up, forever demanding justice and never listened to, not by our parents when we were children, and not by the adult that we have become with time. *Perhaps in the end, all forms of psychopathology represent the outcry of a lonely child who has never been heard and who is continuously and forever crying for justice by means of 'vengeful hope'.*[24] The answer to the question raised above is rather simple. As I have already stated in Chapter I, pre-conceptual traumas split the mind in two states, the 'traumatised' and the 'non-traumatised'; the former is structured by unthought-of thoughts or beta elements which could only be used as material for projective and introjective identifications; the latter, on the other hand, represents the progressive mental growth of any individual, and is controlled by the alpha function capacity to change beta elements into the alpha elements that can be used for thinking. *When our mind is ruled by the traumatised state, we might act and use mental logics similar to a child's thinking, just as we did in the past, when emotions determined our actions; while at the same time, communication with the exterior is made with the use of projections that always change present reality into a past time.* It is possible someone might ask: 'Well, what is new about this?' I would add that this form of epistemological confusion is, and always will be –some more, some less – ubiquitously present *in all existing human beings*, regardless of being considered normal, neurotic, or psychotic. As a matter of fact, such classification is based on the quality and intensity of the pre-conceptual trauma.

---

24 About 'vengeful hope', see Chapter V.

How children think

Distressing reality will always prompt in children, as a form of defence, a sequence of mental mechanisms: a need to repress, to split and project these unpleasant emotions, and to use magic and omnipotence as a form of defence to deal with their helplessness. The main purpose of these mechanisms will be to destroy the link between both: the sensory experience from reality and the emotion elicited by that experience. Such disconnection, however, will stay forever, and when we grow older we might remember the fact, but will not recall the emotions that remain repressed. This condition will make it often difficult for the adult to match the specific emotion with the sensory impression that originally triggered it and to which it was once attached. The repressed and disconnected emotions would then be able to unconsciously link to any other traumatic event that might take place in the future once we have become an adult, but never with the original situation responsible for its creation in the past. It is usually with the help of psychoanalysis that it is eventually allowed to find its original roots. It is because of this mechanism that transference and countertransference exist, as well as projective and introjective identifications, paranoia, self-envy or the phenomenon I have previously described (López-Corvo, 2014) as '*trauma entanglement*'.

A clinical example could be useful. Julian is forty year old medical doctor, married with two children, the oldest of three siblings, the younger being a sister and the middle one a boy who died in a car accident two years ago. At the beginning of the session, he said that he is a bit anxious, because he is not very happy with the administration of the hospital where he is working and had applied for a position in another institution. He already had one interview for the new job, but had received a call from them requesting another interview with the director of the hospital. After a short silence, he continued and said his mother had asked him to accompany her to see her financial adviser, because she is very ignorant about money issues and his father had recently separated from her and had moved to another city. I wondered about what could have made him associate the search for a new job with his mother requesting him to accompany her to the financial adviser. I then asked him what he thought the director of the hospital was going to ask him, that made him so anxious. He replied that he did not know, and I added that the director was perhaps like a 'father figure', who he feared was going to inquire about his present position in relation to his mother, because he had managed to get rid of his younger brother when he died, his sister was living abroad and his father had deserted his mother; a series of incidents that had made him his mother's 'adviser' without any rival. He thought for a moment and then said that he remembered when he was five years old his father was jailed for three years in his native country due to political reasons. 'I remember becoming my mother's help because I was the older, and I thought then that I was happy because my father, who I was afraid of, was gone.' I said that his present situation was similar to what he experienced as a child, because his father was absent, his younger brother dead and his sister away, that perhaps he feared that this new 'father director' who is now requesting to interrogate him may find out his murderous phantasies in relation to his father and siblings in order for him to become his mother's only advisor.

As is well known, Jean Piaget is well recognised in psychology for being able to discern all the secrets prevailing in children's cognitive thinking. Piaget (1965) described, for instance, an experiment with a ten month and eighteen day old child: 'while the child observes, Piaget twice hides an object in location A and waits; the child then looks both times in A and finds the object. He then, pretending that he is hiding the object in B, withdraws it and hides it away. The child then looks in B, but when he cannot find it he then returns to location A to look for it!' It is an action that reminds us of the old expression 'looking for the key at the wrong place'; or, in relation to this experiment, 'looking for the object at the original place'. This type of confusion can also be observed in the transference, when patients 'look for' their parents or siblings in the therapist, by unconsciously projecting ancient and repressed feelings that were once experienced with their parents. It is also a common conflict of communication among couples, of how they continuously confuse each other with their own siblings and repeat between themselves their own childhood feelings of sibling rivalry. A womanising man, the third boy after two girls, was always trying to find in all women the unconditional love he might have not received from his own mother, who changed her attitude towards him after a second boy was born and he was no longer considered the 'male heir' to the family. Piaget also refers to a situation, similar to the previous one, where a one and a half year old boy was playing with his mother in the garden when suddenly his father appeared and walked closely to the child. He sees the father and smiles while the mother asks: 'where is daddy?' and, curiously, instead of pointing to his father who is just in front of him, he turns immediately to the desk where his father usually sits. They repeat the situation a few minutes later, with the father standing a metre away from the little boy, and when the mother says aloud the father's name, he turns his head to the place where the desk is.

There are other circumstances I consider of great importance because of their relevance in psychoanalytical technique. I am alluding to the impossibility to pinpoint or describe events that have taken place at too early an age to be remembered or named. Consequently, they cannot be recalled spontaneously into consciousness, although they can be acted out or experienced by means of projective-introjective identifications, as observed in transferencecountertransference interaction. It is not a material for thinking – as stated by Bion (1957) – and can only be organised as sensations or perceptions undistinguished by the patient from dream stuff or from transference and countertransference, during the psychoanalytical practice. They represent split undigested stored facts or beta elements that become minutely split and are then projected, via projective and introjective identifications.

Let's take, for instance, Piaget's distinction between two forms of imitation: '*immediate*' and 'differed' or 'representative'. The first type is present in the early stages of development when the child is not yet capable of internal representations and imitation is reproduced by observing and replicating the *external object,* just as would a monkey. The second form of imitation demands a process of consecutive introjections where imitation would be fed and determined by *internal representations,* resulting from previous successive imitative incorporations. I believe that the '*immediate*' type of imitation represents the main mechanism present in patients in whom the traumatised state is characterised by 'as if', or 'false self' type of personality, as a kind of 'chameleonic' imitation in a form already described by Deutch (1942), Winnicott (1951), Bick (1968), and Meltzer (1966), among others. The '*differed*' type of imitation, on the other hand, will be related to disturbances of the true process of identification, like negative Oedipus or gender confusion.

A clinical presentation might be useful. I have previously stated that often when parents fail to follow children's form of thinking they resort to 'adultisation', meaning that they treat them as pseudo-adults. Beatrix, a thirty-four year old single woman in analysis for the last three years, was the consequence of this kind of traumatic abuse. She consulted because of 'too much stress from work'. From the beginning she appeared as an 'as if' personality, always ready to please others without ever considering her own needs or having the right to make herself present. She gave the impression of being driven by fear, feeling that unless she pleased she would not be loved but completely rejected instead; a threat that induced her to become the other person's desire and to feel and act such desire, as if she was a prisoner of that desire and did not exist by herself. As a result of this attitude, she was usually abused at work because, out of terror for being totally excluded, she found it extremely difficult to refuse when asked to perform tasks that were beneath her responsibility. Afterwards however, she felt angry at herself for being such 'a coward', while at the same time she was too afraid of protesting and felt very stressed due to the amount of extra work. There was the countertransference feeling that something happened early in her life that prevented her from achieving an inner sense of selfness.

Beatrix was the oldest of three children, with an immediate sister and a younger brother, over two years apart from each other. I mused whether she, being the oldest, was forced by her mother into the role of 'helper'; however, since she was just a baby, she often failed and was reprimanded by an angry and impatient mother. Following Piaget's concept of 'immediate imitation', she has remained fixed in those first years of her life, duplicating others – possibly her mother – from a distance. It seems as if there was not an emotional nearness that could have created in her a sense of belonging, or immediacy, as if she was forgotten, ignored, in total anonymity and continuously feeling 'two children away' from a 'contemplative imitation'. This early environment did not provide her with the capacity to feel that she had the right to *exist* at her own will, but only to imitate the other, to exist by proxy. Beatrix's attitude is reminiscent of Walt Whitman's poem (1855) "*Leaves of Grass*", when he said:

There was a child went forth every day; And the first object he looked upon...that object he became; and that object became part of him for the day, or a certain part of the day, or for many years, or stretching cycles of years. [p.106]

Bick (1968) had referred to the skin as an organ that envelopes the body and binds together parts of the personality providing differentiation or a boundary between internal and external spaces; however, '...this internal function of containing the parts of the self is dependent initially on the introjection of an external object... Until [these] containing functions have been introjected, the concept of a space within the self cannot arise.' The differentiation or 'skin' separating the self from the object will result from the introjection of an especial object Bick believed to be breast. Failure in the creation of this primarily Bick's 'containing object' will induce a 'frantic search for an object – a light, a voice, a smell, or other sensual object' representing a 'secondary skin', which will then act 'momentarily at least, as holding the parts of personality together'. (p. 484)

Beatrix felt that everything was too much for her. She was either anxious because she might not be able to deal with her work demands, or she convinced herself that she was not capable of doing so. After some time it became obvious that she also feared her own aggression. Her younger brother committed suicide when she was seventeen years old and she felt extremely guilty, sheltering the unconscious fantasy that she might have something to do with his death. A year ago, just one month before the anniversary of his death, she suddenly produced a delusional and paranoid idea that she was going to be fired from her work, that her boss was building a case to get rid of her, that she was going to become unemployed, penniless and had decided to end her therapy. I said to her that she was in the process of firing herself from work and from her therapy, on the verge of her brother's death anniversary, possibly because she felt so guilty that she decided to torture herself as a form of punishment. In her mind, either to make herself present as an individual, or to 'murder', were the same thing. She said 'yes' to anybody's request because she felt unconsciously that to say 'no' was an act of 'deadly' aggression. It was a powerful dilemma: to make herself disappear by becoming the Other's desire in order not to kill – possibly her mother – or to murder the other by making herself present; it was absolutely one or the other possibility without any other option. It is a kind of ambivalence that sometimes reaches extreme levels of action, more often seen in men than in women in the form of 'serial killers'. There is in these men the unconscious need to murder their own mother projected in any woman, and then, out of extreme guilt and in an effort to disavow their action, they bring them back to life as if they have not committed any crime, becoming afterwards ready to murder again, in an endless circularity.

Chapter IV
TRAUMATISED STATE AND ITS COMPULSION TO REPEAT, AS A FORM OF DEFENCE

> *The main purpose of analysis would be, to dismantle the demonic compulsion of the 'pre-conceptual trauma' to continuously repeat itself, and being able at the same time, to promote the 'non-traumatized state' to take over.*
>
> — R. E. Lopez-Corvo

In *Remembering, Repeating and Working Through*, Freud (1914) introduced the concept of 'repetition compulsion', which he considered was an acting out that represented a form of remembering, that was taking the place of memory. In addition he also stated that it was the 'expression of the most general character of the instincts, namely, their conservation'. Green (2002) elaborating Freud explained that,

> The compulsion to repeat has to be understood...from two angles: as the impossibility of giving up immediate satisfaction; and, since the level of frustration is intolerable, as a violent expulsion from psychic space in a mode reminiscent of action. [p. 78]

TRAUMATISED STATE AND ITS COMPULSION TO REPEAT

Freud's theory of instinct has been very much questioned, possibly, as Meltzer (1978) once commented, because this theory was perhaps the expression of a 'bad influence', resulting from Darwin's Theory of Evolution. Addressing this controversy I have previously said the following:

> The difficulty in using a model of the human mind based on Darwin, as Freud did, pivots on the lack of discrimination between humans and animals. We might be born with naked drives searching for satisfaction, similar to other animals, but immediately after birth, a *realisation* is established with the proper object, say the breast, and the drive will no longer remain divorced from that particular experience; or in other words, from the very beginning, the instincts had become attached to specific objects, as we learn from the experience. Fairbairn (1952) summarised this in his well-known statement, that 'libido [aggression too] is object seeking' (p. 82). Different from what Freud had established, Klein and her followers affirmed that instincts are not entelechies that can exist free from experience and that could easily detach themselves from the object in order to invest in the self (secondary narcissism), but they are emotional incidents that remain firmly fastened in 'constant conjunction' to all objects of experience that remain stored as memories or beta elements. They are, as Bion stated, 'pre-conceptions' or states of expectation searching for realisations, like undigested facts that remain amassed in the mind as 'beta elements'. [López-Corvo, 2014, p. 28]

The compulsion to repeat represents an on-going mechanism used in the 'traumatised state' as a mode of controlling the mind, which, at the same time and as a consequence, submits the adult's emotional judgement completely under the supremacy of a child's logic, resulting in acute mental suffering and sometimes even death. Similar to what cancer cells do to normal cells, 'repetition compulsion' abducts the 'non-traumatised state' and prevents the use of alpha function or 'logical thinking' as the only instrument able to craft an inner state of well-being. It is then obvious that the main purpose of psychoanalysis and psychoanalytic psychotherapy would be to dismantle this demonic apparatus.

There are reasons why the 'non-traumatised state' remains passive, and unable to make use of logical thinking, in contrast to the powerful control exercised by the 'repetitive emotional child elements' present in the 'traumatised state'. By failing to provide logical meaning to the 'repetition compulsion', the mechanism that sustains the traumatised state is always responsible for psychopathology's perpetuation. It seems as if the ego subordinates itself to the traumatised state, and remains passive and indifferent to the continued mental suffering induced by repetition compulsion. I often make interpretations to demonstrate that the important matter is not so much the emotional confusion itself, or whatever symptomatology the individual is experiencing, but the fact that they do not assert control and take ownership of their own issues; instead, they remain passive and wait for something or someone to rescue them.[25]

In relation to the physiology of the 'repetition compulsion', it is important to question what exactly is being repeated, and why there is such a continued obstinacy to repeat. In answer to the first question, I put forward that it is the *pre-conceptual trauma* that continuously repeats. *Why* it repeats might not only be the product of the instinct's compulsive need for satisfaction, nor the attempt to remember something that has been forgotten, as Freud has stated,

---

25 See Chapter VIII.

nor an instinctive need to master 'wild thoughts', as other psychoanalysts – like Hendrick (1942) – had established, something I have previously questioned (López-Corvo, 1980). I don't deny that some of these mechanisms could also be present in the process of compulsive repetition, but I think they are not the main reason. I would like to consider that perhaps the most relevant mechanism present in the compulsion to repeat, is similar to what Bion (1967) once referred to as 'hallucinations', 'a magic and omnipotent defence against frustration'. In other words, what is at stake is not so much 'a pleasure-seeking mechanism', but a 'defensive purpose'. This aspect can often be observed when patients recreate the whole scenario, not only their defence but also, and very importantly, the reason for that defence, a condition that represents the main dynamic that structures the transference.

A clinical presentation could help to follow this theory: Josephine was a fifty-three year old, married patient, the only girl and oldest of three children, who grew up feeling very isolated and lonely. As a child, she felt envious of her twin brothers who seemed to draw especial attention from her aggressive and very religious mother as well as from her mostly absent father. At the time of this presentation, she was extremely anxious because she was to undergo a surgical intervention to remove some polyps from her intestines, and she feared they might be malignant. Her oldest daughter, someone she always relied on, had recently married and moved to another city. She started the session complaining bitterly about her husband, accusing him of not helping her around the house, as if he did not care about her. She also complained about her absent daughter, whom she felt was indifferent, and about a neighbour's friend she considered selfish and envious. I had the feeling she was trying to get my 'support', by showing me how terribly lonely she felt, for being mistreated by her husband, daughter and friend. I thought, with the pending operation and possible diagnosis, she was feeling very threatened and lonely, similar to how she felt as a child. Perhaps the lonely child in her felt envious of her husband and friend, because they were fine and free of worries. She remained silent, tears rolling down her cheeks. She said that she was feeling very lonely, possibly like she felt as child. I then said that she was worrying herself, because, after all, there was no certainty that she had cancer, that she had to wait for the surgery, but what could be malignant was her unconscious need to torture herself by reproducing the loneliness she experienced as a child by attacking people who were emotionally close to her, and to fear that they could get angry and retaliate by turning against her. In summary, an internal malignant mother was inventing a 'diagnosis of cancer', which filled her with despair and envy towards those who surrounded her, whom she attacked. She unconsciously felt that by doing this she was going to convince 'the father' she had projected in me that she was in distress, and that I would protect her from feeling so lonely. The truth was that all she was going to accomplish was to induce more loneliness by turning the people who loved her against her.

In summary, what endures, repetition compulsion, is a primitive defence against castration anxiety, not only genital castration, but any form of aggression experienced by the child as a threat to their life and to their well-being. In his theory of thinking, Bion (1967) established that when a child has a desire for an object and that object is not present, there could be at least three types of reaction: i) the frustration for the absence is tolerated and changed into a thought that will modify the frustration and make it more tolerable, allowing the ego to learn from experience and to make use of language; ii) if the frustration imposed by the absence of the desired object is not tolerated, the mind will block any form of logical thinking and will try to rid itself of the bad experience, by means of massive projective identifications; iii) *the frustration intolerance is dealt with through the use of omnipotence and omniscience* (p. 114); this third option is of great interest in my interpretation, because magic and omnipotence are very often used by children. Taking this last explanation into account, I will say that the mechanism that sustains 'repetition compulsion' is produced by the patient's inability to give up a strategy the child considered a successful 'omnipotent mechanism of defence' which was employed to shield them from environmental threats that induced feelings of fear, helplessness, anxiety, and loneliness. I can think of at least three main mechanisms supporting the repetition compulsion: i) 'trauma entanglement', ii) 'self-envy,' or envy between the parts, and iii) 'vengeful hope'. About 'trauma entanglement', I have previously published a paper on the subject (López-Corvo, 2013); however I will summarise the concept now for the purpose of this chapter. 'Vengeful hope' will be described in detail in Chapter VII, and 'self-envy' will be considered in Chapter XII.

Trauma entanglement

'Trauma entanglement' is a link between the present and the past. It represents the tendency of traumas from the present time, or 'conceptual traumas', to perpetually trigger 'pre-conceptual traumas' (López-Corvo, 2013, 2014). In other words, whenever an actual situation induces a sense of hopelessness or loneliness, the whole omnipotent defences that were used as a child and were then thought as peerless, will be relived in the present, in an ongoing and endless fashion that feeds repetition compulsion.
To summarise this mechanism we will have to consider a series of related steps: in the first place, there is in all children a biological sense of helplessness and *loneliness*, which will induce a need to idealise their parents as possible rescuers; however, these parents are also at the same time the main source of menace from whom the children want to be res-

cued. Such a condition will induce a splitting of the parents' imago, in good and bad parents, producing feelings of ambivalence. The intensity of this ambivalence would be directly proportional to the intensity of the aggression exercised by the parents. At an adult age, this feeling will be repeated and will participate in the control and polarisation of the ego because the contradiction and intensity of the existing emotions involved will produce either 'guilt' when there is retaliation against the 'bad parents' – usually using omnipotent phantasies – or anger against themselves, once they please and comply with the 'loving parents'. Perhaps some clinical vignettes could be of some help.

Case 1: a woman in her early fifties had already been in psychotherapy for several years at the time of her consultation. She was the oldest and only girl of three children. In the transference, a condition became obvious through a circular dissociation between an envious and aggressively daring part of her and a very critical and cruel superego; she was both the angry child who protested and the critical and unfair mother who punished her. Often in her sessions, and as part of a repeated pattern, she would struggle with whether to tell me or not of how critical she had been of me, of my office, or what I had said to her; then she would express about how terrible she felt for being so critical. I always reassured her that she hadn't done anything to me; that they were only words, possibly from a lonely and mostly powerless child element in her, who repeated a pattern not only because she was unable to remember painful memories from her past, but also, and very importantly, because it was a mechanism she had used as a child, when she felt so lonely and so powerless. However, after a while, it became clear that the compulsive repetition of her criticism, together with my own interpretation, demanded further understanding. I considered that she was displeased by the thought that her words had no effect on me. She was simultaneously feeling two opposite emotions: guilt for being so critical, but also the desire that her words carried enough power as to truly belittle and control me, possibly representing what she might have wished to do to her parents when she was a helpless little girl. I felt she was struggling with a deep and very primitive sense of loneliness inside of her by using two different defences: anger for feeling so abandoned, which induced her to be envious and critical, while significantly at the same time emboldening 'the helpless little girl' who wished her thoughts and words were truly powerful and a magic weapon of destruction. In the transference, she felt guilty for being so critical, but at the same time, to acknowledge that her criticisms were not striking, she left the little girl in her completely powerless and trapped in an endless circularity, and, as a consequence, extremely lonely; it was a condition that many patients strongly resist, inducing them to reject therapy. To my surprise, her insight about this contradiction resulted in an opening in the compulsive circularity of her primitive and omnipotent defence. She became less anxious, and, in turn, more aware that her use of infantile defences was completely anachronic, because at the present time she was a powerful woman who had no need for it.

Case 2: John is a forty-five year old man, the oldest of three siblings, four years older than his immediate brother, married with two small children and in analysis three times weekly. He started the session by saying that lately he has had more difficulty remembering his dreams, and that perhaps what I have said to him before could be true: that he produced dreams for *me* and not for him, that possibly the envious little boy in him was trying to attack me by not remembering his dreams. I said that what he said made sense. Often, while I am giving him an interpretation, he produces images of me in what he felt were demeaning situations, like me performing fellatio on him, or him having anal intercourse with me. I interpreted that he continuously reproduced the same situation that he might have experienced as a child with his powerful father. He conceived of himself as a 'powerless and impotent child', while at the same time reinvented me as an authoritative and dangerous father whom he had to attack using *silent* but degrading and omnipotent phantasies about a powerful penis. In order to invert the situation, and to neutralise the terror of castration he once experienced from his father, he felt he had to make me helpless while he exercised absolute control. He then remembered a long dream that portrayed his oedipal anger and sense of helplessness. '*My wife and I are in a hotel room. We were having sex and having a great time. It felt like we had been there for a while. Suddenly there was a knock on the door and my wife's ex-boyfriend walked in. At first, we got along and all was fine, but I started getting annoyed that he was there and asked him to leave. He did not want to go. We struggled and fought and I was able to push him out of the door and closed it. There was a hole in the middle of the door, perhaps a mail slot. He put his hand through the hole and opened the door and came back in. I called security and the guard came into the room and went very aggressively toward the ex-boyfriend. He tried to force him to leave and they started talking. Suddenly, the security guard was laughing and became friendly with the ex-boyfriend. I was angry, wondering what was happening. More hotel employees came in and they all loved this guy. They then turned and left the hotel room with the ex, and as they were leaving, they looked at me like I was the asshole. Before they left though, my five year old daughter showed up in the room.*"

He said his dream was from last Sunday, after his wife's relatives were at his house for the weekend. Among them was his sister-in-law's husband, whom he finds rather aggressive and arrogant. I said that I wonder if his presence could have triggered his dream, that perhaps he reminded him of his aggressive father. He agreed and I added that his daughter was in the dream to possibly indicate his age when similar things took place between him and his parents or after the birth of his younger brother, at the time that he was having 'a great time' with his mother and father, but which was interrupted after his brother was born and he became his mother's 'ex-boyfriend'. He became dejected, helpless, and extremely lonely, possibly because everybody liked his new brother so much and he felt that he had nobody to turn to.

Chapter V
LONELINESS IS IN THE HEART OF PRE-CONCEPTUAL TRAUMAS

> *And he said: 'I tell you the truth,*
> *unless you change and become like little children,*
> *you will never enter the kingdom of heaven.'*
> — **Jesus, in the Gospel of Matthew: 18:1-4**

> *'Illi mors gravis incubat, Qui, notus*
> *nimis omnibus ignotus moritur sib.'*[26]
> — **Seneca**

Children's *loneliness* and *helplessness* are the main fuel that drives the Oedipus complex, representing the need in any child to be rescued from feelings of isolation, helplessness and exclusion, the need of finding a saviour, usually the parents, who, being motivated by their own particular essentials and process of identification, have already expressed some preference: like the father who favours his daughter, or the mother who prefers her son. At the same time, the siblings and the unchosen parent become a hindrance, like the enemy that must be 'eliminated', a condition that

---

[26] 'What a sad death awaits, to who, being well known to others, dies not knowing himself.'

induces unconscious guilt, need for forgiveness and terror of being punished, emotions that also amount to a sense of guilt and loneliness, as we shall see in Chapter XI on envy and self-envy.

There is a difference between *loneliness* and *aloneness*; the former is a subject related to psychopathology, the latter to existential philosophy, like in Heidegger's concept of 'Dasein', meaning to be 'abandoned there' by our own implicit nature, to be completely on our own, like 'a leaf that falls from the tree'. *Loneliness* is an emotion associated with unresolved primitive feelings of dependency or neediness, as experienced in childhood, because children are not emotionally capable of 'loving' their parents: they 'need' them; while parents, on the other hand, would be capable of loving them. *Aloneness*, in contrast, refers to freedom, independence, and is associated with the adult's capacity to *love* and to be *alive*:

> But to be alive in the manner I am now advancing here, does not necessarily refer to the quality of being endowed with life, as it happens with animals or plants; it requires more precisely a full awareness of being a 'living human being'. What then does it mean to be alive? It means the presence of an intuitive awareness of selfness, uniqueness, autonomy, continuous growth and, paradoxically, a sense of deadness. It requires a denotation of unconditionality, to feel that you could be loved for what you 'are' and not for what you 'have' or for what you 'do'. [López-Corvo, 2014, p. 10]

Loneliness as a singularity is more regarded as transcending the present situation, as a form of regression to primitive conditions containing loneliness. One can feel lonely even if there are many people around, or one can be completely alone without feeling lonely. Loneliness can disappear with a sense of belonging, when one links with a 'rescuer', much like how we felt as a child when our mother was present, or, as adults, when our mind is dominated by the traumatised state and we meet someone whom we unconsciously confuse with our parents.

'Love' and 'need' reveal similar inclinations; however, they are completely the opposite in their final purpose. Need is a child's emotion and is also present in the 'traumatised state' within any adult's mind. 'Love', in contrast, is always the product of an adult's mind, or, to be more specific, of the 'non-traumatised state' within the mind of the adult. I have previously said that the meaning of love is

> ...to be aware of the 'other' as someone different from oneself, as a complete human being who cannot be possessed and by whom we cannot be possessed either. Love always elapses within the boundary of absolute freedom and is always a voluntary decision that arouses unrestrained without any other alternative. Love is never abrupt because it is always chiselled by time and history, is particular, personal, private and *never anonymous*. Need on the other hand, determines the interaction from the children towards their parents – although never the opposite – or between master and slave; is immediate, imprisons and suffocates the person, is *always anonymous* and the expression of a deep feeling of fear, dependency, insecurity, and spiritual disadvantage. In other words, *love liberates but need oppresses*. [López-Corvo, 1997a, p. 140]

Love also allows us to share, without losing our independence or individuality, in total freedom of expression and in complete power of our actions. Need, on the other hand, shatters the boundaries between oneself and the other, inducing symbiosis and maintaining the primitive infantile relationship between the mother and her child. 'Love,' said Spanish philosopher Ortega y Gasset, 'is an exchange of aloneness.'

Pre-conceptual traumas are structured as an onion, made of different but associated superimposed layers of events, which can be successively exposed during the analytical process in order to reach the *essential*, which is often organised following a tied, high speed, circular argument between dialectically correlated opposite emotions. The most common emotions I have found in clinical work that assembles the *core* of all pre-conceptual traumas, are not only *helplessness*, as Freud once stated, but also *loneliness*; it is usually structured by a tied, fast, circular, emotional and dialectical argument that denotes a deep sense of desperation and absolute loneliness. The sense of *loneliness* that often assaults us as adults could very well be a reflection from those early years of our life when we thought and spoke using a different language and lived in a dimension – as Saint-Exupéry brilliantly described in "The Little Prince" – that was not only dissimilar from our parents' but also not understood by them. The problem, as I will often reiterate in this book, is that this child's outcry of loneliness will continuously repeat inside of us in many ways, because, just as our parents failed to understand us as a child in the past, the child who is now inside of us ('traumatised state') is still unheard, misunderstood or unrecognised by the adult ('non-traumatised state') that we are now; or the problem may manifest as the opposite, as an envious attack by the traumatised state over the adult part, or non-traumatised state, by ignoring and disregarding any adult judgement or capacity to think logically. Mechanisms of the latter kind can be considered a form of self-envy and are often observed in patients who start therapy with the unconscious purpose of 'testing' the therapy, as if they were expecting some kind of magic intervention to solve all their troubles, while simultaneously attempting to enviously prove that the therapy will always fail. Some vignettes might be useful.

i) In a previous work I referred to a woman who, at the age of three, was placed by her mother with a stranger family, in order to hide her and protect her from being abducted by her father from whom her mother had been divorced. She consulted because progressively, and due to different reasons, she had been experiencing serious enmity towards most of her family members, leaving her rather emotionally segregated. It seemed as if, unconsciously, a part of her was continuously re-creating her placement by provoking relatives and friends to the point that she was feeling emotionally isolated, similar to when as a child she was placed and living with the strangers; an emotional condition that induced in her the need for someone to 'rescue' her. However, at the same time, anybody capable of becoming emotionally close enough to display the characteristics of a true 'rescuer' – like her mother was at the end of her placement – aroused suspicion in her as she associated them with the 'placing mother'. This feeling induced her to rapidly and aggressively move away. It was a circularity produced with such speed that it was difficult to see the mechanism with a 'naked eye'. Any loved one was at once, a 'rescuer-placer', a contradiction that left her absolutely paralysed, hopeless and completely lonely. (López-Corvo, 2014)

ii) A young patient who consulted because of depression, suicidal ruminations and chronic use of pot, was the middle child of three siblings. He felt his older brother was preferred by his mother, while his younger sister was his father's favorite; it was clear that, by being in the middle, he considered himself the forgotten one, who – as he stated – 'fell into the crack'. It was obvious that his suicidal contemplations and his use of marihuana were the consequence of a deep sense of loneliness, mostly due to his father. I have often expressed that drug abuse is directly proportional to the 'excesses of mother and the absence of father'; in other words, the presence of the father is absolutely indispensable to protect a teenager from the abuse of drugs and for being sequestered –as Meltzer (1992) stated – in the mother's anal claustrum. At the beginning of his therapy and within a short interval he brought up three dreams, always remarking on his sense of loneliness and hopelessness, mostly in relation to his father: a) *He is trying to get into the subway, but realises that he does not have enough money to buy a ticket, then his father suddenly appears, coming from inside the train, sees him and walks away without saying anything.* A week later he had two dreams: b) *He is at home and one of his friends is trying to kill him; his mother is watching but his father looks indifferent;* c) *His grandfather finds pot inside a peanut butter can that the patient has put inside the Frigidaire and he shows it to his father, who says nothing.*

Detecting childhood loneliness in the transference

We can often distinguish signs of childhood loneliness in adult patients' transference-countertransference interaction: a forty year old married man, the older of two children, consulted because of chronic anxiety and frequent bouts of depression. He revealed that his parents got divorced and his mother abandoned the family when he was nine years old. Often, as he started the session, he would endlessly complain about his boss, his wife, and other members of his family, about how he has been misunderstood, unfairly accused, or how they continuously made demands of him. In the countertransference, I experienced the need to always take his side and to talk against whomever he was complaining about. I had the feeling that this mechanism showed that he might have experienced his loneliness as a child, possibly when he visited his mother and complained about his father, as well as the opposite, when he returned to his father's place and complained about his mother. In other words, he was looking for someone to take his side and to be emotionally close to him.

An opposite interplay is seen when patients attack themselves with the unconscious purpose of being rescued. By showing signs of loneliness they induce in the countertransference a need to save and protect them. During the first session following one week of holiday, a young woman in her second year of analysis stated that she wanted to say something nice to me, to welcome me, but her feelings then changed and she said that she felt terrible and wanted to commit suicide. I felt that for the first time in her analysis she allowed herself to be nice and to welcome me with gratitude, and to let me know how pleased she was to see me again, as if she had made room for the *hope* of a warm relationship based on forgiveness. However, in the silence of her pause her anxiety appeared, and with it came the envious and destructive attack from an internal narcissistic element that closed the 'opening' and cancelled the possibility of giving in to the compromise of a good working alliance, of a creative harmony and a *depressive hope*. I said to her that she seemed to be confused as to what to give to me, whether to provide me with a nice welcome and to let me know how happy she felt to see me again, or to make me feel terrible, perhaps because of the anger she may have experienced from my absence. 'I feel terrible,' she answered, crying bitterly. 'I am always doing it wrong, I am always destroying. I am good for nothing. I don't want to do that to you.' Countertransferentially my feelings changed and, instead of the anger I experienced previously, I felt the desire to hold and calm her. I said to her that it might have been difficult for her as a child, due to her anger, to express directly to her 'abandoning' mother her immense need for her, and that unconsciously it was easier for her to attack herself in order to induce the mother then, and me now, to be nice to her. I also said that she was struggling inside with the loving feelings she had for me, as if an angry part of her felt envy toward a loving part inside of her. The conflict was not so much with me, but between two different parts of her.

The core of the pre-conceptual trauma continuously reproduces itself in a tied, rapid and unconscious argument that recreates the past, in the form of an 'emotional trap', that even if we are always the one who unconsciously recreates and reproduces this trap, we are also never able to avoid falling into it! It is this dynamic that we will be considering in the next chapter.

Chapter VI
THE 'TRAUMATIC TRAP'[27]

The Traumatic Path and the Onoda's syndrome: or 'not being able to acknowledge, that you have already become an adult'!

The traumatised state represents, following Bion, the world of beta elements which are 'minutely split' – or 'atomised' following Ferenczi – and then projected everywhere, like missiles, together with the mind that contains them; a mechanism that with time will structure a world of ghosts and lies in the form of projected bizarre objects and dream furniture, similar to what Plato described in the "Allegory of the Cave". For instance, there is the tendency in all human adults –whenever their mind is contained by their traumatised state – to unconsciously feel and act in relation to themselves and others as if they were helpless children who remain forever surrounded and threatened by a never ending number of powerful and dangerous parents, projected everywhere. I refer to this situation as the 'Onoda syndrome', based on the true history of a Japanese soldier with that name, who refused to believe that the war had ended and that he was no longer a 'fighting soldier' surrounded by powerful enemies.[28] It is like an intra-psychic drama whose screenplay and characters were established in childhood,

---

27 A version of this chapter has been published in the 'Revista Catalana de Psicoanalisi', Vol. XXXIVI/2, 2017.

28 Hiroo Onoda was a Japanese soldier who continued fighting World War II for the unbelievable time of twenty-nine years after the Japanese had surrendered, because he stubbornly refused to believe that the war was over. He was sent in 1944 to Lubang Island in the Philippines with other soldiers to fight guerrilla war and never to surrender to the enemy. He continued through all those years attacking local farmers, killing their livestock and fighting the police as if they were still his enemies. He always

but are now continuously repeated using the same script but with a new cast of characters by means of projective and introjective identifications, similar to Pirandello's play "Six characters in search of an author". These mechanisms can be found in all sort of psychopathology, although more easily observed in the transference. In summary, there is in all existing human adults an unconscious denial that we have grown up and that we are no longer the emotional and confused child we used to be, but instead we continue to act out as an adult, as if time has not elapsed and we are still a child, similar to what Onoda did when he stubbornly denied that the war had ended.

Specifically, the 'traumatic path' corresponds to how the pre-conceptual trauma within the traumatised state is capable of *replicating* itself in such a disguised and perverse manner that it manages to deceive the non-traumatised state into making it believe that it is avoiding the suffering involved, when in fact it is participating in reproducing it. This path is unconsciously and continuously 'sold' by the traumatised state to the non-traumatised, as the true way out of mental pain; however, the real truth is that paradoxically this path is exactly the course that leads to the hub of the pre-conceptual trauma, the place of suffering, anxiety and despair; because this condition will perpetuate the repetition of the pre-conceptual trauma, and will precisely make it the real trap.[29] It is a trauma that contains the paradox of being completely

---

disregarded leaflets announcing the end of the war because he was convinced they were enemy tactics to get rid of him.

29 Qin Shi Huang (259 -210 BC), China's first Emperor, feared death and was obsessive and desperate to find the fabled elixir of immortality; however, paradoxically he died at the age of forty-nine after ingesting mercury pills made by an alchemist in order to make him immortal. I can think of another useful paradoxical allegory: in India, there is a tradition often used by local people in order to capture a monkey. They tie a coconut shell to the trunk of a tree, make an opening in the shell large enough to place a nut inside, and wait. Once the monkey becomes aware of the nut,

saturated but in continuous search for a saturation that could never be saturated! After all, with time, these confused emotions from childhood that structure the pre-conceptual trauma become, following Freud, unconscious feelings that repeat compulsively, making it difficult to use alpha function to question and change them for other ways more adapted to the adult's present reality; besides, after several years, the original causes of the pre-conceptual trauma have already been repressed and defences have become automatic. In other words, the pre-conceptual trauma is structured as a tyrannical presence of historical absences that consolidates as ego and superego identifications (or *identificate* using Sohn's suggestion),[30] which establishes how the ego and super-ego interact. An important part of the ego and superego would continuously follow the *path* that has been determined by the configuration of the pre-conceptual trauma, something reflected, for instance, in the phenomenology of the transference-countertransference interaction.

Some clinical vignettes might be useful: Patty was an attractive, forty-three year old woman, the only girl and the middle child of three siblings. Her mother idealised her brothers, while at the same time projected on Patty her own debased image for being a woman. This condition induced in Patty a sense of self-devaluation for being a girl, and, as compensation, a prevailing phallic envy, which resulted in different forms of acting out, like stealing (mostly food), and eventually bulimia.

---

it puts its hand through the hole and grabs the nut, but since its fist is larger than the opening, it cannot withdraw its hand without giving up the nut; however, because the monkey will never let go, it becomes trapped by its 'hunger and stubbornness'.

30 Sohn (1985) has used the word 'idenficate' as a noun to designate internal elements resulting from identification process. Although it is not a word normally used in English, it is common in languages originating from Latin or Romance languages, like '*identificado*' in Spanish, which can be used either as a reflexive verb or as a noun.

Case 1: A woman in her mid-fifties, the oldest of three siblings and married for the third time, sought consultation because of marital difficulties. She complained about her husband's compulsive work and emotional distance, giving the impression that she was on the verge of a possible third divorce. She had previously seen other therapists but always interrupted treatment because she felt disappointed by them. There was the presence of a narcissistic superego structure conceived as a kind of ideal ego or idealised model, possibly resulting from unresolved oedipal conflicts, which continuously made sadistic demands of perfection in others, as well as herself.[31] About two years into her analysis, she made up her mind and left her husband to stay at her parents' house; however, several months later, she decided to return to him. This became an important experience that helped her realise that her conflict was not only external, with others, but also inside, within herself. She was not happy with her husband, but she was not happy without him either. She became aware that such a cruel demand for perfection was really an attack against herself, to her own well-being, because, if she was to continue in that hopeless and endless quest, she was going to end up completely alone. As the analysis progressed, it became clear that such continual pursuit was a defence to cover up an immense oedipal envy towards a 'harmonious couple'. The envy she might have experienced as a

---

31 Idealisation is often connected to anal fixations and toilet training. Within the dynamics of the pre-conceptual trauma, soiling often becomes an instrument of attack or debasement among siblings. Later on the correlation between 'clean and dirty' changes homeomorphically (López-Corvo, 2014) into other endless dialectics, such as good and bad, beautiful and ugly, intelligent and dull, idealised and debased, and so on. At the same time, the bad or debased is always projected using projective identifications while the opposite – good idealised – is introjected; however, since defence mechanisms are never perfect, such projection-introjection will always fail and, because it is most of the time unconscious, it will need to be repeated again and again.

child towards her parents' affectionate relationship she was now experiencing within herself, towards the couple she was now capable of creating as an adult with her own partner. All of her life she had acted out the belief that, if she was to attack her own 'harmonious couple' created with another person, or to project her harmonious couple and to attack it in others – like her marital and analytical couples – she could set herself free from the terrible pain of her own Oedipus exclusion. It was a circular mechanism, meaning that she was never capable of realising that, by placing herself outside her own internal rejected or abandoned elements, she was always going back to the hub of the conflict. The result was not only that she remained always isolated, but also and as a consequence extremely envious of the harmonious couple she had projected on the others!

There is another aspect to consider, representing a defence to castration anxiety (superego threat), which could be regarded from different vertices; for instance, the dread towards 'emotional dependency', sensed as a form of vulnerability that will induce the use of projective and introjective identifications to place the dependency on the analyst and to make the analysis completely irrelevant. In this case, for instance, the patient could be late, miss sessions, delay payment and often even interrupt therapy. The other vertex I have observed, which is used to deal with castration anxiety, is the need to deprive animate objects from any form of life in order to exercise a total control. The use of some clinical material could be of some help.

Case 2: A twenty-seven year old patient who, at the age of six, went through a painful surgical intervention, finds it now very hard to deal with her depression, sense of helplessness, transference disappointment and anger, as well as the feeling that, to do something for herself, on her own, would involve facing her suspicion that 'nobody cared'. It stems from what she experienced while in the hospital, when she could not figure out why her parents 'hated her so much'. Perhaps it was because she was 'unworthy, unlovable and guilty of something she had never been able to understand', that she was 'severely punished' with a painful surgical intervention. To take over and look after herself, to protect herself from her own sadistic superego attacks, represented the insurmountable task of giving up her endless unconscious hope that her parents – mostly her father – would come to rescue her. Perhaps to do nothing and to wait in despair was the right thing to do, because it would provide her with a way out, the hope that someone who loved her dearly would set her free from the pain of an ongoing surgery that seemed to be haunting her everywhere. But when this possibility was presented, she would then attack it in her mind out of envy and revenge, and destroy it again and again, leaving herself always in the midst of her painful and hopeless 'surgical intervention'. It would be better to keep alive the hope that the father would come and finally rescue the abandoned and tortured little girl, than to go ahead as the adult she is and rescue herself from the predicament of a tyrannising absence in which she endlessly placed herself. Such a perplexing drama is always at the bottom of any serious pre-conceptual injury, as observed in borderline pathology, or as in self-envy mechanisms or negative therapeutic reactions.

Case 3: Regina was a forty-five year old married architect, the oldest and only girl of four children, who grew up feeling abused by her depressed mother and her constant demands from her to not only to look after her younger siblings, but also after her angry father. In the majority of her sessions she would cry bitterly and often complained about feeling mistreated by her husband and her stepdaughter, while at other times she accused herself unfairly for any 'wrongdoing'. In the countertransference I felt forced to take her side and to protect her not only from others but also from herself, as if she was an abandoned, desperate and lonely child in a permanent need to be rescued. Whenever I tried to make an interpretation in this sense, she reacted very angrily as if she refused any form of insight about her condition and stubbornly defended her need for me to side with her in a protective manner against her 'accusers'. I said that, similar to what she might have experienced with her father, she would like me to team up with her against all others, which quite possibly represented her mother and siblings.

Recently she had been complaining about how her husband and his daughter seem to have some kind of 'romantic relationship', and usually behaving in her presence in such a 'lovey-dovey' way that it seemed the main purpose was to exclude and anger her. As usual, I sensed she made these statements as a kind of projective identification, attempting to make me side with her against them. I wondered why she was so jealous of someone like her stepdaughter, who, being completely forbidden to her husband, could never have replaced her. Perhaps she was confusing her stepdaughter with her own mother and her husband with her father. It was as if she was struggling with an emotional memory that she could not remember, a memory of how angry and envious she might have been as a child when she felt that her father, preferring her mother over her, was being 'lovey-dovey' with her. In the subsequent sessions she continued struggling with the same feelings: angry at her husband and her stepdaughter, feeling threatened by their closeness, and angry at me for not overtly taking her side. I then started to wonder about the stubbornness of her defence and why her non–traumatised state completely failed to contain the traumatised one, of the absence of an observing ego capable of finding in the analyst an ally who was trying to rescue her from the trap of the powerful control exercised by a pertinacious and repetitive pre-conceptual trauma. I then said to her that her main dilemma, and what she really feared, was her capacity to discriminate between herself and her stepdaughter, by which I meant to convince her that, like her stepdaughter, she was never a true threat to her own mother. It was all or nothing, or the certainty that she could really have her father – or the analyst – all for herself, or that she could have nothing at all. If fulfilling this oedipal desire was not possible for her stepdaughter, it meant that it was not possible for herself either! It was like losing all hope completely and eternally.

Case 4: A young woman, the oldest of five children, became deaf because of a viral infection when she was very little, and her parents ignored her condition until she was almost three year old, once she evidenced speech limitations. She often acted out revengeful and deadly impulses against her parents, often disconnecting her hearing aids and remaining lost and isolated in a world of total silence. She grew up feeling left out and suffered, on and off, from ulcerative colitis, which she associated with her parents going through a chaotic divorce when she was around ten years old. Other times she played for hours in her room with stuffed animals representing her murdered parents, which she could talk to at her leisure; an exercise that made her feel good. This was also evident in the transference as a need to control and relentlessly attack the interpretations by 'hearing but not listening'. She often ignored what I said and only paid attention when she was talking but not when I interpreted. I was the 'stuffed' analyst she never listened to, but would continuously talk to. At a given moment, she referred to a friend who was a vegetarian, who 'doesn't like the veins and bones because it makes her disgusted and red meat gives her diarrhoea'. I said that perhaps she feared finding spoils from her murdered parents that she continuously cannibalised and then freed herself of the remains anally by means of her colitis. We could say that this mechanism represented a way to liberate herself from the terrible pain induced by the existence of unconscious tyrannical ghosts of 'present-absences' or 'no-things'. I said to her that her main problem with her symptom was the befuddling of making her rectum an organ of phonation, by mixing up 'v' with a 'b', meaning 'bowels' instead of 'vowels'!

Following Klein (1946), different forms of split emotions within the paranoid-schizoid position, like feelings produced by the presence of the 'good-idealised' part-object as well as the presence of its absence or 'bad-persecutory' part-object, represent *opposite emotions that correlate*. If a part-object symbolising the presence of the absence or bad-persecutory contains, for instance, a sense of 'being left out' or excluded, the good-idealised might symbolise a sense of 'inclusion' or importance, and there will always exist a correlation between the opposite emotions present in these two part-objects, emotionally attached but separated in distance: if the 'exclusion' is projected, the 'inclusion' will be introjected and vice-versa. I refer to this combination of both emotions, which are *opposite* and *correlate*, as *'bivalent part-objects'*.[32] These part-objects represent preconceptions in search of a realisation – like a moth to the light – by means of correlation. Someone who feels intra-psychically the pain of 'exclusion' will search for somebody who acts as important and 'included', with the *envious* purpose of inverting the situation. Following the specific emotions present in every person's pre-conceptual trauma, there will exist different forms of correlating pairs as well as the specific penumbra of emotions

---

32 See López-Corvo, 2014, Chapter XI.

associated with them: masochist-sadist, voyeur-exhibitionist, rich-poor, dependent-independent, significant-insignificant, courageous-coward, nun-prostitute, and so on.

There is another important aspect to consider: there exists in all humans the unconscious need to reproduce via projective and introjective identifications the image of the 'rescuer', what Ferenczi depicted as the *wise baby* and Beckett immortalised as 'Godot', signifying the representation of the primitive parents. The conflict with this representation is that it contains ambivalent emotions, because these original parents were at the same time the main source of pre-conceptual traumas as well as the rescuers; it is the fabric that structures the superego and outlines the transference as a trap. A clinical vignette might be useful.

Case 5: A woman consulted because progressively and, according to her, due to different reasons, she had become chronically depressed, a condition she felt was leaving her rather emotionally isolated. This condition became more obvious after her mother's death six months previously. She remembered that when she was around five years of age she was sent away to live with her maternal grandparents in a different town, until she was nine years old. From the very beginning it became obvious how resentful and envious she felt towards her entire family, with the exception of her mother towards whom she always appeared very considerate. When exploring this matter, she also stated that she never got angry at her mother, until she experienced a serious anaphylactic reaction following food poisoning. I interpreted that this incident made her feel for the first time what death was about. After she went to live with her parents, she feared expressing anger, because if by doing nothing she could be sent away, imagine what could happen if she acted out? She feared her mother could have even killed her.

In the transference, there was always the feeling that I was the one who had all the answers. She asked about what I said, but seldom gave her opinion, as if she wanted me to always tell her what to do. I felt that I was the master and she was the servant who felt completely ignorant. I said she deprived herself of any value, and gave it all to me, like the relation between a little girl and her parents, where she knew nothing and they knew everything. She went to visit her grandmother who accused her of being too naive and that she, the grandmother, knew better. This infuriated her. She felt that her grandmother was acting just like her husband. I said that she sheltered in her mind two opposite feelings: on the one hand, she attempted to make people believe she knew nothing, while at the same time she reacted with increasing anger whenever she felt that someone, like her grandmother or her husband, was putting her down. She felt terrified of having a mind of her own, of having her own judgement; it was as if she felt that to think was to be criminal and dangerous because it could trigger the possibility of 'being sent away'. The other possibility was that perhaps an unconscious part of her felt she had killed her mother and was trying to bring her back to life by knowing nothing, never thinking, just disappearing as she seemed to do with me. *If I think, then I am alive and she is dead, or placed elsewhere, but if 'she thinks', I will be dead like her mother.* This thought terrified her. It is like either one plus zero, or zero plus one, but never one plus one; if one is, the other is not, like all or nothing, only one knows because the other is zero, a 'no-thing.'

In the next session, she complained about feeling very *lonely* because her husband, who was ill, was demanding and failed to recognise all that she did for him. I associated her *loneliness* with what she could have experienced as a child when she did not feel 'validated' (an expression she had used) in how she had suffered when she was abandoned by her mother and stayed with her grandparents. I said that it was difficult for her to know if her sense of loneliness and lack of validation was produced only by her husband's attitude, or if it was also an emotional memory from her childhood's abandonment. In the next session, she arrived very late and after a long silence said that she felt I was like something that held her together, like a backbone, and that I had become essential in her life (she cried). I felt she was plucking petals from a daisy: 'love me, love me not'. Forgetting was a way of getting rid of me, while making me her 'backbone' was like bringing me back to life again. It might have been similar to the extreme ambivalence she could have experienced as a child, towards her mother, because she was the 'placer' (forgettable) and at the same time, the 'rescuer' (backbone).

A total incapacity to question the nature of the conflict is also frequently observed in such patients, because the ego very often surrenders passively to the control of the pre-conceptual trauma. In other words, it is the superego that is always *silently* questioning the ego, using a modus operandi summarised in the always accusing and paradoxical dictum of 'damned if you do, damned if you don't'. The opposite, like the ego rebelling and inquiring about why the superego is at all times viciously accusing and threatening, is very seldom exercised; possibly because the ego, being contained by the pre-conceptual trauma, always reproduces emotions resulting from the interaction between a helpless little child and his or her powerful and ordinary parents. It seems as if the ego being hostage to the superego behaves in a manner similar to the 'Stockholm syndrome',[33] passively adapting to the 'superego kidnapper' without ever questioning its action; after all, psychoanalysis entertains the purpose of taming the superego with the use of the interpretation, in order to make it – with time – less cruel and less unfairly demand-

---

33 This is a very important aspect that is further investigated in Chapter VII.

ing. These conclusions are extremely relevant because they depict the existence of an alive dialectical system that reproduces part-objects intra-psychically, between the ego and the superego. A dynamic that can also be observed in the transference-countertransference dimension, where the same emotional interaction that once took place between the child and his or her parents is again reproduced. In other words, the process of identification represents an alive dialectical system that remains always active with the use of projective and introjective identifications.

Case 6: A man consulted due to a *consecutive* crisis of insomnia, paralysing bouts of anxiety and a sense of persecution usually precipitated whenever he felt threatened by someone he sensed as being too hostile, dishonest or manipulative. He recounted his seven-year-old daughter being very anxious when awakened from a bad dream in which her mother appeared as some kind of a monster. He consoled her until she went back to sleep. The problem, I said, wasn't that perhaps he contained inside his mind an angry and threatening mother-part that terrorised him, but the absence of an element that could wake him from his nightmare and console him into quiescence. Perhaps he also felt so ashamed and angry at himself for being so 'terrorisable' that he judged himself, similar to how his father/mother did, as if he were an ashamed, frightened and castrated little boy.

He often defended himself using self-flagellation as a form of projective identification with the purpose of being rescued. He endlessly complained about his work, how he experienced insomnia, depression, paralysing terrors, while at the same time he accused himself of procrastinating on his duties, wasting time on nonsense, and feared being fired. At a given moment, he shared a dream: *he was in front of his boss who was saying all sorts of terrible things about him, that he was careless and lazy, that his work was sloppy, and so on. Then suddenly, a distant man from the crowd started to scream about the boss: 'Don't believe him! You don't have to believe him! Why does everybody believe him?'* He associated his boss with his father and the continuous accusations and demands he made on himself; and I added, 'Who is now inside your mind?'

Such accusations of deficiency represented how his father had communicated with him (positive link), and were now reproduced as a kind of false or negative link, revealing how his super-ego relates to his ego. A new and emerging change was indicated by a shift towards using positive links: were the screams produced by the internal object represented by a still '*distant* man' (whom he associated with the analyst), who demanded to know why the super-ego (boss) was not questioned? Why was he not more loving (positive link) and understanding towards himself, now that he was an independent and resourceful adult? Why did he not question his internal parents instead of repeating the way he was originally treated by his accuser father and the disinterested mother who failed to wake him up from his continuous nightmare?

At the beginning of this chapter I have referred to different unconscious strategies the traumatised state uses in order to control the non-traumatised state. One of these tactics is to encourage the use of the 'traumatic path' as the only hope to achieve a state of well-being, by means of a hope that is based on revenge or 'vengeful hope'. This is an important and essential mechanism that I will be considering in more detail in the next chapter.

Chapter VII
VENGEFUL HOPE vs. RENUNCIATION HOPE

> *When embarking on a journey of revenge, dig two graves!*
>
> — Confucius

Historical Hope

Just as individuals adhere to a system of beliefs, so too do cultures throughout the world and time. The direction and outcome of civilisations has been shaped by the sets of 'hopeful tropisms' that people believe and would follow, determining since primeval times the outcome and direction of civilisations. For ancient Egyptians, for instance, hope was based on the attainment of immortality, not to die, but to continue living eternally, to travel with their Pharaohs in magnificent boats through the limitless lands of the infinite; although only the Pharaohs were preserved, because the common people could reach the heavens just by proxy. All that we know of them today is a direct consequence of relics they fashioned in pursuit of this powerful drive. For the Hebrews, hope was based on the fostering of a direct relationship with their monotheistic God, to be chosen as the elected people, to be unique. The appearance of somebody being called the true Son of God, which was exactly what everybody might have hoped, could have induced massive envy, which I think was perhaps the case with Christ. For the Greeks, on the other hand, hope was based on the quest for knowledge, on a rational comprehension and exegesis of Nature; whereas the Romans privileged power and domination above any other human appetite. Hope became the corner-stone of Christianity, mostly based on eternity, inspired by the Egyptians, but with the difference that, for the latter, it was necessary to preserve the body. The Christians, following the customs of the Hebrews[34] – their older brothers – not only privileged the soul, making superfluous the preservation of the body, but, unlike the Hebrews, widened the access of God to any believer, a democratisation which resulted in the preference of burial instead of pagan cremation and, subsequently, to the appearance of the Romans' catacombs. The other important aspect of the 'Christian hope', was repentance with the use of regular confession, a practice taken from the Hebrews' 'Day of Atonement', although extended to everyday. Religion also sustained the purpose of hope through the Middle Ages and the Renaissance, meaning to be good even if hypocrisy was necessary, to be immaculate in order to reach the eternal life and the abundance of Paradise. Christ introduced three important changes to his own Judaic religion: i) the democratisation of God by relinquishing 'uniqueness', as seen in Judaism; ii) complete forgiveness through confession and repentance, regardless of the size of the sin; and, most importantly, iii) the promise of Paradise and eternal life. With such offers, Christ and his disciples became the greatest merchants of illusions of all times; ever since, Christians' hope sold around the world like hot cakes!

With the 'death of God' proclaimed by Nietzsche and other nihilistic philosophers – such as Heidegger and Sartre – during the end of the last two centuries and up to the present one, the relevance of life after death, as well as the powerful control and dominion of the church, started to fade away, slowly inducing the appearance of a need for an earthly and epicurean enjoyment, not of the spirit, as professed by the Greek philosophers, but of the

---

34 See Tobias, N. C., 2017.

senses, to do it all while you are still alive, because there might be nothing after death. According to Existentialism, a philosophical understanding of mankind which dominated the last century, men were forced to hold themselves to the only thing that was left: their disillusionment for living, and to feel that to exist humanly they ought to accept, with tragic resignation, the commitment of creating every day their own reality, under a Godless sky and within a senseless world. Conceived without any determination, man is just an accident, whose life is spent *chasing days by fulfilling 'mean-whiles'* and who is fatalistically doomed to die. This is why modern hope is based mostly on personal pleasure and enjoyment, 'narcissistic' as many have referred to, with little restrain, fast money, personal power and a full experience, including, money, sex and drugs, to do it all and to do it for me, today, because tomorrow might be too late. It is the age of *'narcissistic hope'*.

Hesiod's Hope

The Greeks who explained mental riddles using myths had produced, by the hand of Hesiod, the myth of Pandora, which we could summarise as follows: Zeus the God of the Olympus created men but refused to provide them with the sacred fire. Being deprived of this necessity, men died of hypothermia; created once more with the same dispossession, they also perished. Fearing that they could have the same outcome for the third creation, Prometheus, the son of a Titan, decided to steal the sacred fire and give it to the man. Enraged by this defiance, the revengeful Zeus decided to punish the people using Prometheus' brother Epimetheus who, although warned by his brother not to accept any present from Zeus, responded to Pandora's seduction and accepted her box, which, once opened, released all the virtues that were inside back to the Gods, except for the *elpis*, the hope, that was trapped in the bottom to remain grounded among men forever. At the same time, as a form of revenge, there were all sorts of plagues also released, such as diseases and death that were not present in mankind previously.

There is an old proverb in Spanish that says: 'men propose, women decide,' something I interpret as the capacity of women, more than men, to unconsciously decide the possibility of structuring a 'reproductive couple', something based on a woman's aptitude to symbolise the Oedipus trap and to fashion in her mind a differentiated *space* that could allow for the existence of a man, who, different to her father, could become a procreant. Most of all, mothers would provide life and 'unconditional love', while fathers would bestow hope and freedom.

We are created within our mother's entrails and remain thus for nine months, as if we were another of her internal organs. Birth arrives and we achieve the biological status of being 'another' individual (undivided), absolutely different from our parents, but only from a biological dimension because, from a psychological vertex, we remain dependent for many years. The continuous process of complex 'bio-psycho-social' maturation and symbolisation (motion, speech, conceptualisation, mental growth, and so on) relentlessly moves us towards further states of autonomy and freedom. Since it is difficult for children to create by themselves a mental space to help them escape from the pull of the maternal natural symbiosis, the father will usually function as such a force, capable of neutralising the mother's gravitational pull. This is why there is the expression that the 'phallus introduces the symbol,' whereby the symbol signifies the successive process of introjection, identification, representation, and autonomic behaviour; or, in other words, '*freedom*'. Meltzer (1992) referred to metaphorical spaces or *claustrum*, inside the mother's body, where her children may remain mentally and figuratively 'confined' forever. He described three of them: i) head/breast, ii) genital and iii) maternal rectum. I believe however that, from a clinical point of view, there is always a combination of all of these possibilities with a predominance of one claustrum over the other. This subject is examined in detail in the next chapter.

Pontamianou (1997) has acknowledged that Hesiod did refer to Pandora's Box as a *Pitos* (Πιτοσ) meaning an urn or tomb where human ashes are kept,[35]. She said:

> The hope detained by Pandora in the obscure depths of her bodily jar surely has to do with the representation and the fear of the maternal power. [p.7]

The 'maternal power' could be interpreted as the 'power' or tendency mothers have to withhold their children beyond their biological needs; after all, there is only a difference of one letter between the words 'tomb' and 'womb'! In contrast, the father will pull the child from the mother, but eventually, not being familiar with the experience provided by pregnancy, he will let the child go. It is a difference already present in Pandora's and Prometheus' myth, where the former retains the 'hope' 'in the obscure depth of her body', while the later provides the 'freedom' symbolised by the sacred fire.

---

[35] In Latin 'hope', 'wait', 'despair', and 'hopelessness' all have the same root: *Spe*, as in *espes, spero, despero y desperare*, respectively. In other words, to wait (spero) means to have hope (spes), where despair (despero) implies the opposite, to lose it all, total hopelessness (desperare). In English, hope originates from the German word *Hoffnug*, an expression that carries no relation to derivatives such as to 'wait', or 'despair'. According to Hesiod, Hope was the only beneficial divinity that remained on the Earth; all the others have left and returned to the Olympus, such as 'Good Faith', also Temperance, as well as all the Graces.

The place of inclusion

All existing human beings have been, are, and will always be fatalistically marked by the indispensable presence and eventual disappearance of primary part-objects, related to both parents. First and foremost the mother, and subsequently the father, are mutually essential; the mother for survival and, by way of unconditional love, the attainment of a sense of 'being human' (animate);[36] the father, on the other hand, not having a uterus, lacks the capacity to withhold like mothers do, and are able to provide *independence, freedom and hope*. Many of these 'present-absences' are temporary events, but many others will overcome Freud's 'protective shield' or Bion's (1962, p. 36) 'maternal reverie' and become permanent, amounting to an enduring distressful search or 'psychic trauma'. The particularities related to these traumatic 'present-absences' will mark each and every individual in a unique manner, eventually becoming a kind of organiser or 'selected fact' that will always establish a particular script to the narrative of the Oedipus complex, as well as structuring the specific demeanor and idiosyncrasy of every existing human being.

There is always a substantial longing for the 'lost objects', and sometimes there is the illusion of hoarding them inside, bringing about a sense of triumph and contempt. At other moments, there is the impression of failure to contain the 'present-absences', inducing a sense of hopelessness and melancholy as well as envy towards those believed to have them. A middle aged woman, the oldest of two girls, who consulted due to frequent

---

[36] Unconditional love is *only* granted by the mother during the first years of life. The only other possibility is that of the adult individual, of being able to display to themselves a similar unconditional disposition, similar to Obermann's statement: 'For the universe I might be nothing—for myself, everything' (cited by Unamuno, M., 1954, p. 47).

bouts of depression and alcohol dependency, managed to associate her emotional crisis with the time when she, at the age of eight, was sent to stay for over a year with her grandparents who lived in a different city. At the time she presented a form of furunculosis or succession of boils, which re-appeared several years later when she was eighteen and had moved abroad in order to continue her studies and felt very isolated and extremely lonely, since, not only did she not know anybody, but she did not speak the language either. It was then that she started to use alcohol to deal with high levels of anxiety, a situation that represented a repetition of her longing for the absent mother, which she experienced at the time when she went to live with her grandparents. The furuncle infection was interpreted as a form of masochistic call for love and help, when as a child she felt that she was sent to stay with her grandparents because she was 'not good', while her younger sister, who stayed at home, 'was preferred'.

The inner void of these absences is minutely split and becomes continuously projected everywhere, pressing for an all-pervading search *ad infinitum*. With age, inner representations of these absences mutate, changing only their 'appearance', in a fashion that emulates the Greek God Proteus;[37] however, the original significance of the absence is always preserved and lingers well-fastened to the primal loss. Based on these dynamics and using Freud's original discoveries as well as Ferenczi's and Bion's contributions, I would like to privilege the significance of 'psychic traumas' and rather refer, parodying Bion, to the dichotomy between a *'trauma tised and non-traumatised state of the personality'*.

---

37 In the Odyssey Homer recounts how Menelaus, who was lost in the island of Pharos after returning from the Trojan War, discovers Proteus' secrets from his daughter. Menelaus manages to trap the God – who had the capacity to take the shape of any object – even after he tries to avoid being caught by successively changing into a lion, a serpent, a leopard, a pig, a tree, and even water.

Hope in Psychoanalysis

Since hope is a necessary concept in understanding important aspects of human behaviour, it would appear rather controversial that there should be so little psychoanalytical literature about its meaning and relevance. It was not mentioned by Freud, and even Bion, who has been perhaps one of the psychoanalysts who has given pertinence to other concepts such as faith, for instance, says nothing about hope. Boris (1976) has stated the following:[38]

> If one searches the standard psychoanalytic literature (I have in mind, for instance Freud, A. Freud, Fenichel, Fairbairn, H. Segal) one is apt to find little in the index between 'homosexuality' and 'hysteria', save 'hunger'. 'Hope' itself is nowhere to be seen. [p1]

From a Freudian point of view, the mind is guided by basic instinctive forces which continuously strive for pleasure, and where pure 'instinctive satisfaction' represents the main path, purpose, or 'hope' that continuously prompts the ego to follow. The libido in Freud's case, said Fairbairn (1952), is primarily a 'pleasure seeking' mechanism. For Klein and followers, on the other hand, it is the specific relationship with a particular object – the breast being the paradigm – that forcefully guides the ego: the libido, in this case, is predominately object-seeking. This, I think, epitomises an important difference between classical theory, represented by 'Ego Psychology' and the 'Object Relation' model. It was humanly impossible for Freud to re-examine during his life time, the vast number of discoveries he was piecemeal bringing to light. Any changes introduced by other psychoanalysts after Freud, in relation to aspects of least transcendence, have added to psychoanalytical practice and

---

38 See: Akhtar S. et. al., 2015.

created little discrepancies. However, those of greater importance – in theory as well as in practice – such as *narcissism, death instinct* or *impulse theory* have been responsible for causing great turmoil, inducing such enormous worldwide incongruities within many schools of psychoanalysis, responsible also for important splits in several psychoanalytical associations. What an inconvenience that Freud was not able, during his life time, to solve completely all the riddles of the unconscious, instead of leaving us to struggle with that heritage of tearing apart and parcelling the mind. Like the descendants of Charlemagne, it is still challenging, in the mind of many, to be able to reach a solid agreement and be competent to benefit from *one true and holistic conception of the mind*. There are still many psychoanalysts who insist, like in Buddha's parable of the elephant and the blind men, on dividing the mind in bits and who will often refer to 'Freudian', 'Kleinians', and 'Bionians' as if they were different religions.

Hope Metapsychology: Normal and Pathological Hope

The dictionary describes hope as 'a feeling of expectation and desire for a particular thing to happen'. The purpose of hope will differ depending upon which mental state rules the mind, either the traumatised (child-like) or the non-traumatised (adult-like). From a metapsychological perspective, such 'expectation' could aim at two opposite intentions. The first purpose corresponds to the 'pathological hope' linked to processes like the 'traumatised state', the schizo-paranoid position, unresolved oedipal conflicts, pathological splitting, narcissistic object relations, and, most of all, associations with strong feelings of revenge that I have referred to as '*vengeful hope*'. The second form of hope is related to the 'non-traumatised state', to the depressive position, reparation, renunciation, and creativity, to which I have referred to as '*renun-*

ciation hope'. This kind of normal and hopeful waiting is possibly related to preparation for death and finitude, with successive renunciation and a capacity to adapt progressively to the continuous becoming of life itself, and with the progressive entropic metamorphosis towards nothingness. It will be impossible to touch on this kind of hope without getting involved with the complexity of philosophical speculations and existential argumentation. Depending on which state controls the mind, whether the 'traumatised' or the 'non-traumatised',[39] the aim of hope will change. If the 'traumatised state' rules the mind, hope would be based on a prevailing ambivalence between *revengeful* and *perverse acting out* towards intrapsychic parental imagoes – continuously projected everywhere – for not allowing infantile oedipal desires to be fulfilled. This form of 'vengeful hope' is always associated with guilt, anxiety, depression and masochistic punishment, because it is a type of hope that will never provide an exit to suffering and is always destined to failure and to continuous repetition; it is also this incessant failure that prompts feelings of 'hopelessness'. Notably, it is this type of false hope that is used unconsciously by the traumatised state in order to deceive and dominate the non-traumatized state, in a fashion similar to what others like Meltzer, Steiner and Shon had previously noted:[40]

> Sohn refers to an 'identificate' that acts similar to the 'pied piper' and intends to lead healthy parts to destruction; Steiner

---

[39] From Klein's perspective, we could similarly discriminate between the 'paranoid schizoid' and the 'depressive' position, or between the 'psychotic' and the 'non-psychotic' part of the personality from a Bion's vertex. Because of conflictive confusions with clinical psychosis in the past, I have preferred to change Bion's concept of 'psychotic and non-psychotic parts of the personality', into 'traumatised and non-traumatised states of the personality'. See: López-Corvo 2014.

[40] See: López-Corvo, 2014, p. 118.

stated that '...a narcissistic part of the personality...can acquire a disproportionate power by gaining a hold on the healthier parts of the personality... does this to the extent that it can persuade these parts to enter into a perverse liaison.' Meltzer also stated that, '...the destructive part of the self presents itself to the suffering good part first as a protector from pain, second as a servant to its sensuality and vanity, and only covertly—in the face of resistance to regression—as the brute, the torturer.' [López-Corvo, 2014, pp. 117–118]

Within the 'non-traumatised state' the hope is based on resolution, reparation, creativity, and the forsaking of oedipal expectations by process of symbolisation, a course I refer to as '*hope by renunciation*'. (López-Corvo, 1995; Perez-Morazzani, et. al. 2017).

Hope also has a defensive aspect, a manic and narcissistic protection against reality, caused by the ego's low frustration tolerance in the face of object loss. It is a sort of delusional system where a situation is fabricated using magic and omnipotent thinking, with the purpose of diverting the ego's attention from a *frustrating reality* to a false expectation, in the form of a denial of reality and a retreat to a narcissistic shelter. It can be observed, for instance, in the final phase of some terminal diseases, in religious or other forms of esoteric belief, in primitive societies or in extreme conditions of confinement.

The scarce psychoanalytic literature is more familiar with the normal aspect of hope, but little has been said about its pathological side, linked with a powerful process of revenge, as can be observed more obviously in the narcissistic structure of borderline psychopathology. There is a significant difference in how the mind, dominated either by one or the other state, will interact with reality and the implementation of hope. The non-traumatised state, using logical thinking, is capable of discriminating between external and internal realities and harvesting hope by renouncing or giving up any form of *desire*; the traumatised state, on the other hand, strives to continuously reproduce the original traumatic situation or pre-conceptual trauma, as if it was driven by an established script, similar to a moth's compulsive search for the light. The hope that dominates this state is based on a desire for revenge against internalised oedipal parental objects, always resulting in unconscious guilt and masochistic punishment; continuously prompted by whatever might have taken place within the heart of the 'pre-conceptual trauma'. In normal hope, the intention is directed not only towards reparation of the breast, but also towards the capacity to transcend such reparation. All forms of hope are present in all existing individuals, although the prevalence of one over the other will depend on the dialectical interaction between the intensity of the pre-conceptual trauma and the aptitude of the ego to deal with frustration. I do not believe that there is a dialectical correlation between a 'normal' and a 'pathological' state. Following Bion, I think that the difference is instead based on the capacity of the 'non-traumatised' to contain the 'traumatised state', qualitatively as well as quantitatively, inside the mind of any existing human being.

Some clinical vignettes might be useful: Peter is a patient I have previously referred to. He grew up in a rather primitive and aggressive environment. He consulted because of the guilt he was experiencing after the death of his younger brother in a car accident. There was a significant amount of repressed violence, not only towards his siblings, but mostly towards his punitive father and his rather indifferent mother whom he felt had not protected him from his father's hostility. In the transference, this anger became obvious through ongoing fantasies he produced in his mind any time I made an interpretation. There were mostly fantasies of me performing fellatio, mutual anal penetration, or even coprophagia, that stemmed from the powerlessness of an angry child who had no other form of defence or revenge other than to produce these fantasies in order to silently and 'safely' attack his violent parents in the privacy of his mind; it was the only hope of a defenceless and lonely child. The problem, I said to him, was that this inner revengeful child he sheltered now inside his mind, who was able to provide *hope* to him when he felt so deserted as a child, was no longer needed. There was no one threatening him now, and, as an adult, he was quite capable of protecting himself. Without being aware of it, he was still relying on this 'revengeful child element', so far legitimised and tolerated, which controlled his mind without him ever questioning it, as if the child in him did not know that he was already an intelligent and powerful grown-up. I felt that the adult in him ('non-traumatised state') would have to introduce himself to the internal ignorant child ('traumatised state') in order for the adult element to acknowledge the dangerous presence of an emotional 'child fossil' still present in him; it was a situation that reminded me of what I refer in Chapter V as the 'Onoda syndrome', exemplified by the Japanese soldier who ignored for twenty-eight long years that World War II was already over! Another important issue was that by attacking me he was mainly attacking himself, because, after all, not only was I not his angry father, from whom he felt he had to retaliate, but I was someone he had 'hired' to help him! The 'revengeful child' that in the past used to provide him with a 'vengeful hope', as he silently struggled against his angry parents, was now attempting to destroy the hope of the adult in him, possibly as a form of 'self-envy'.[41]

---

41 I have previously referred to self-envy (López-Corvo, 1992, 1995, 1999, 2003) as a condition resulting from an envious interaction between different part objects composing the Oedipus structure. Let us suppose, for instance, that there is an important increment in the amount of envy that a child, who is feeling excluded,

I had three patients who, for different reasons, shared similar pre-conceptual traumas as well as similar psychopathology.

i) 'A' was the second child born after a sister, in a well-to-do Muslim family. He was led to believe he was going to be a sort of 'heir Prince'. However, when he reached the age of five, a younger brother was born and the family's original fascination with him shifted completely towards the younger boy.

ii) 'B' was a boy who was born two years after his older brother died at the age of one year. His parents, as well as his grandparents, turned to B as if he was the 'replacement' for his dead brother, perhaps as a way of dealing with the difficult and painful process of grieving the baby's death. He was overprotected to the extreme, possibly because they were very frightened that B could have followed the same fate of his older brother. However, this attitude towards B changed once he became three years old, and a younger sister was born; an event that made him no longer the 'only replacement' for his dead brother.

iii) 'C' was a forty-five year old man who had been living in a common law relationship with a woman for the last ten years. His mother was a rather aggressive woman, professional and internationally successful in her profession. His father, on the

---

experiences towards his parents; let us suppose that this envy is mostly directed to what the child acknowledges as feelings of harmony, love, sexuality, creativity, communication, etc., between the couple. As the years go by, these feelings could become idealised and remain in the self as 'foreign' elements not completely assimilated by the ego. When this child grows and becomes an adult, just like his parents were, the unassimilated envious element could again be reactivated, but this time such elements previously envied in his parents are now part of himself. This condition is always reflected in the transference as a sustained attack against idealised links between analyst and patient, experienced as a 'creative', 'productive' and 'harmonious' analytic couple (López-Corvo, 2006, pp. 75–76).

other hand, was rather passive and dependent on his wife. 'C' was the second child after a sister, and he became his mother's favourite child, until another girl was born two years later.

The three cases have in common the inconsistency of two opposite situations: on the one hand the disproportionate presence of their mother, followed, on the other, by an excessive presence of that mother's absence, lacking at the same time the existence of the father as a 'rescuer', for example, 'A' and 'B', because the father was mostly absent and very aggressive, and 'C', because his father was rather passive and dependent, like an older brother. The three patients exhibited in common a significant ambivalence towards women: a powerful 'need'[42] for their love and attention, while at the same time an intense anger and a desire for revenge. For all three it was important that other men were involved and that they may compete with them as an unconscious expression on the presence of an oedipal father. Their main desire, their emotional north, was to find a woman they could seduce and control with their penis, but not with the purpose of loving them, or sharing their lives with them, but to possess, control and disregard them continuously, similar to the way in which they felt their mothers did to them as a child. Their main hope, and what continuously guided them emotionally in life, was just plainly to exercise a 'vengeful hope'. I will clarify these dynamics further in the next entry, about 'vengeful hope and basic delusion'.

'Armando' was a very creative and highly achieving architect, who consulted because of chronic anxiety related to pain in his legs with limitation of movement believed to be related to multiple sclerosis. As a little boy, he experienced a painful and difficult

---

[42] For a difference between 'need' and 'love,' see Chapter IV.

surgical intervention that filled him with anger and revenge. During his analysis, we managed to understand that, as a form of masochistic defence, he resorted to use of his body as the place where he could punish himself, in order to avoid retaliatory castration. There was a significant feeling of guilt, related to hidden revengeful attacks he felt he had produced on the object, by means of his achievements: a kind of 'Faustian sacrifice,'[43] that he subjected on himself as a punishment in order to feel free to exercise his creativity. In other words, his achievements were mostly driven by an unconscious purpose of attacking his parents and siblings, and by inverting the original envy and anger he experienced as a child when he had undergone a painful operation. As a result, the pain in his legs came to unconsciously symbolise his need to paralyse his drive to 'move ahead', as a form of punishment.

Melissa was an attractive thirty-six year old married Venezuelan woman who was dealing lately with very sad memories from early childhood when her parents, who were in the diplomatic service, often travelled, leaving her behind in the care of maids. Those early separations left deep scars: depressive bouts that were often silenced with the use of alcohol, sexual or manic acting out, ambivalent feelings about men, and difficulty in establishing lasting relationships. She had been married four years for the second time – the first time lasting only two years – and has been complaining with certain resentment against her husband, as a possible displacement from her abandoning father who did not seem to be able to rescue her from the depth of her frustrating impotence. She sheltered fantasies of being unfaithful, and of divorcing him and finding someone else. She also complained

---

43 I am referring to the allegory portrayed by Goethe in the Faustian pact. This patient's superego represented the devil, which negotiated unconsciously with him, in order to allow him to enjoy his creativity and prestige but, like Dr. Faust, he was going to pay for such achievements with his body ailments.

very bitterly about his sexual inadequacies, and his lack of ambition in his work. Recently his company sent him abroad in order to evaluate some programmes and, while there, he was offered a possible transfer to England. He liked the idea very much and she referred to it with great pride and pleasure. During the next three sessions she spoke about her plans to take English courses, sell their recently acquired house, and to find a school for her children. She progressively started to degrade and to distance herself from whatever might have to do with Venezuela, while idealising everything foreign. She began missing sessions regularly as she had never done previously.

Some weeks later, she referred to a dream. It was a pleasant dream that she linked with her moving plans: *there was a lovely place. It was like autumn, because the leaves were yellow and brown and it was cold, had to do with England for sure, because it definitely was not Venezuela. There were some ducks swimming in a lake, like they were ready to fly south, and one of them had like a double head, one looked right and the other looked left.* She gave no further associations.

The symbolism of the duck reminded me of the goddess Janus, with her two faces, one looking backward into the past and the other forward into the future. I felt the dream served to denounce her 'false hope' of finally finding an ideal place where all her pain and suffering could finally disappear. It was as if the dream was saying: 'it is fine if you want to migrate and move into the future, into such beautiful illusion; but keep one eye looking back: to the summer, to Venezuela and the analysis'. It was as if unconsciously she recognised her need to create such an illusion as a narcissistic retreat where she may protect herself from the depression, emptiness, and hopelessness she had experienced as a child.

The Dyadic Interaction: 'Vengeful Hope' and 'Basic Delusion'

Two important mechanisms should be considered in relation to 'vengeful hope': one which I had previously referred to as 'basic delusion' (López-Corvo, 1995) is *dyadic*, between the mother and her children, the other is *triadic*, between the child and both parents representing the dynamics of the Oedipal complex.

Men and women use different means to deal with castration anxiety; men use 'competition', to such extreme that very often they produce devastating wars; while women resolve castration anxiety and phallic envy – or the unconscious 'narcissistic absence' for not having a penis – by having babies, preferably boys. The mother's unconscious need to use her child as a completeness for her 'narcissistic absence' induces in the child a feeling of 'essentiality'. However, when she turns to the father, or when another child is born and the mother uses this new baby as a solution to her 'narcissistic injury', the older child will then experience this change as a form of *traumatic betrayal*, together with great pain of *exclusion* and anger towards the mother, as well as the father and the newborn. It is an emotion that becomes the main source for 'sibling rivalry'. Castration will then be denied by believing that if 'I am not the chosen one, someone else would be completing the mother's "narcissistic absence".' I have previously referred (López-Corvo, 1995) to this belief as the 'basic delusion' insofar as it is the belief that someone must certainly be indispensable to complete the mother's 'phallic absence'. This situation also produces in the child a dialectic interaction between 'the presence of the object', or feeling included, and 'the presence of the absence of the object', or feeling excluded, resulting in the need to project the 'exclusion' and incorporate the 'inclusion'. This mechanism promotes great envy and a need for revenge against parents and siblings – always projected on to others – representing the unconscious belief that such mechanism or 'vengeful hope' is the only way out of mental suffering. This 'basic delusion' is essential in the structuring of the main foundation of the Oedipus complex, something I will be referring to in more detail in Chapter X. The mother's need to use the boy for her narcissistic completion – for not having a penis – will induce in the boy a need for her, an interest that will be later displaced to his daughter, inducing in her a need for her father, and afterwards to other men. Christian was a five year old boy when his younger sister was born. At that time, his mother inreferred, he was very much dependent on a security blanket and a pacifier that he continuously kept at hand. The day after the mother came back from the hospital, Christian said to her: 'Mom, why don't you take that baby back to the hospital?'

What complicates this search is the ambivalence between 'need' and 'hate', which is always experienced towards the lost object once it is 'repossessed'; the object is passionately desired when *not* possessed, but always attacked and rejected once 'recovered', in an incessantly and endless dialectical repetition, which always leaves the individual with empty hands and the need to search again. It is an endless loop that supports the illusion of a limitless 'vengeful hope'.

Some clinical examples might be useful: Manuel was a patient with a history of sex addiction, like a sort of compulsive 'Don Juan'. His adopted mother adopted him at birth, because, after three years of marriage, she had failed to have children of her own; however, as is often the case, four years after he was adopted she became pregnant with a boy and two years later with a girl. The contrast between how his mother behaved towards this patient before and after his brother was born was so great that he usually sadly referred to such disparity as the time of the 'prince and the pauper'. An undescriptive envy towards the rest of his family was fostered internally, which afterwards became projected towards anybody whom he considered to be part of a 'harmonious couple', including his own family. It became obvious that, behind his compulsive need to treat women as if they were his enemies, or to seduce them in order to possess them and to subsequently disregard them, was the unconscious desire for revenge against his mother and siblings as a sort of 'vengeful hope'. It was as if there was an unconscious connection between his penis and his anus and, instead of using sex as an expression of love and creative pleasure, it was used as a destructive instrument for vengeance and degradation. This insight was difficult for him to accept because the whole structure of this defence was based on 'all or nothing' or a 'black and white' form of dialectic. He felt happy and in high spirits whenever he saw the opportunity of exercising this vengeful hope against his mother and siblings projected in others, but at the same time he felt depressed whenever he sensed that such an action was not possible. Even more so, when he felt threatened with the possibility that, for the sake of his well-being, he may have to give up what had been a successful strategy, he feared it would make his whole life 'absolutely empty'. However, the reality was different because, in truth, there were serious consequences for exercising his vengeful abuse of women and mistreatment of others. He felt anxious, guilty and often sensitive and paranoid. His family, whom he conceived of as an essential part of his emotional support-system, was often abandoned by him and there were frequent clashes with his wife who had even filed for divorce. Furthermore, his neglected older son was heavily into drugs. What Manuel did in order to free himself from pain was, in actual fact, the exact main reason for his suffering!

Luis was a forty year old business man, who consulted because of 'the stressful situation he was experiencing at work'. He appeared impatient and rather aggressive, having discontinued his therapy twice on account of his travelling often, but wished for me to keep open his appointments while he was away, but not to charge him. At one point, he revealed that a friend he had hired was dishonest and apparently stealing money from the company, and, although he knew that he would have to fire him, it was difficult because of the friendship. I said that perhaps he felt something similar towards me, when he had tried to fire me because he felt I was 'cheating', but found difficult to do so. Luis was the oldest of three brothers and a sister. There was an older son who was born two years before Luis but had died when he was just one year of age. Luis' birth became a relief and a compensation for the pain and bereavement his mother felt from his older brother's death. Fearing that she'd lose Luis too, his parents became totally dedicated to his care and protection, until he was four and a sister was born. The children became further substitutes for the older boy's loss; however, it was not only his mother's change of interest that became traumatic for Luis, but also the fact that she became more and more 'diluted' as each of her other children were born. Life became even more traumatic for Luis at the age of six when another sister was born. He began kindergarten, resulting in tremendous feelings of abandonment and loss of his family's initial attention. This condition became the core of Luis' pre-conceptual trauma. He responded with narcissistic rage and frequent temper tantrums, totally incomprehensible to his parents, who reacted with more rejection, resulting in Luis' further anger and acting out, leading to further rejection from his care-givers, in an endless circularity. As he grew older this condition became more difficult to manage, such that when Luis reached the age of eleven, he was sent away to live with distant relatives in another country, with the excuse of continuing high school. It was a decision that left him very depressed and contributed to his feelings that, while he was once treated like the prince of the family, he was now cast aside, ignored, continuously punished after each successive sibling, and no longer needed for his mother's bereavement. As he grew older, a nameless terror that he could be sent away grew unconsciously in him, to the point that now it was he who was continuously 'sending himself away' in order that he may continuously rescue himself. He had become a very wealthy and powerful man, in his main desire for 'vengeful hope'. By becoming more powerful than his family members, he was no longer the 'vulnerable child' that could be sent away. His parents and siblings would require of him instead, and not the other way around. He had a great need to control others, mostly with money; he would employ persons he knew were in financial distress, and then insist they were abusing him; he would use any inconsequential wrong-doing as an excuse to fire them. It was similar in his analysis, as he was always very late in his payments and became very angry whenever I attempted to raise his fee due to inflation. It was a form of revenge against his internal parents that he constantly projected on others.

The main purpose for this need within the traumatised state, was based on the hope that he may regain the inner sense of 'essentiality' by becoming again the 'essential one' who 'fulfilled his mother's absence' over the father and other siblings; it represented a denial of the castration anxiety as well as a reversion of the painful exclusion induced by his Oedipus essentials. A significant aspect of the ego becomes enslaved to this mechanism, and very important decisions in a person's life are made according to such 'vengeful hope'. The fuel for this hope is envy, based on the possibility of projecting on to the other the sense of 'exclusion', by means of degradation, while attempting to preserve inside the feeling of 'inclusion' by means of idealisation. Such mechanism is unconsciously sold by the 'traumatised state' to the 'non-traumatised' as the only true way out from suffering or 'vengeful hope'.

'Vengeful hope' is also sustained by the existence of a very important paradox that threatens the possibility of fulfilling the *basic delusion* as a trap or a 'catch-22' dilemma: if the mother needs the child to fill her 'biological absence', it will mean that she does not have a penis, that she is in reality castrated; which will also imply that disavowal fails and castration is possible. But if, on the other hand, she does not require the child because she has her own penis (fantasy of the phallic mother) the child is not indispensable and castration is also possible. There is also the presence of a clinical paradox that I have previously referred to as the 'fecal phallus' that I will be discussing in the next chapter.

'Vengeful hope' is also based on the possibility of destroying any rival presumed capable of fulfilling the 'basic delusion' of completing the mother's narcissistic absence, such as a powerful father or a favourite sibling. If the idealised object, capable of making this basic delusion possible, is projected, the attack would be directed towards the external object. If this object is introjected, the destruction would be directed inwardly, against the creative aspect of the ego, using the mechanism we have referred to previously as 'self-envy'.

Hope by Renunciation

What exactly should we forsake? If we think that the 'vengeful hope' is driven by a 'narcissistic fusion', as a compensation for the lost breast, as well as a powerful need for inclusion, revenge and masochistic guilt, then 'hope by renunciation' should be compelled by the freedom resulting from containing and relinquishing those longings. There are several facets to be considered: in the first place, within the traumatised state, vengeful hope characterises a substantial motivator that determines a very significant aspect of our behaviour. Vengeful hope is a consequence of the failure to contain the pain that results from the

VENGEFUL HOPE VS. RENUNCIATION HOPE

loss of primary objects, mostly the breast, due to the ego's poor frustration tolerance as well as the intensity of the pre-conceptual trauma, or both. There is in the traumatised state a continuous longing for the lost object (the breast) as well as the unconscious belief that this lost object could be regained by means of *omnipotent control* of any object where the 'presence of the absence' of the lost object might have been projected. However, as we get older, such objects that have been chosen as spaces for projection would continuously transmute symbolically into other objects, due to the unconscious need to continuously project everywhere the painful and uncontained presence of the absence of the primary lost object. There is also an intense ambivalence towards the breast or lost object, feeling at once the need and the hate in such a way that the breast is relentlessly procured with the purpose of destroying it, in such an ongoing circular rhythm that the lost object can never be preserved. In other words, it is a defence that always fails because what is mostly needed is also hated and always attacked.

An intelligent young man works intensely in order to make himself wealthy, but is never happy with what he makes because it is never enough, so he is always unhappy. A fifty year old woman, a successful actress who was the only child of a well-known actor, grew up feeling very insignificant as she competed with her mother for her extremely idealised father's love. She complained about feeling very lonely after deciding to divorce her husband to whom she had been married for over twenty years; a decision that took place after she had become infatuated with a well-known writer whom she had idealised like her father, although she had never seen him personally and only kept an epistolary correspondence. I told her that she reminded me of Aesop's dog, who was crossing a bridge with a piece of meat in its mouth and saw its reflection on the surface of the water. Believing it was another dog with a 'nicer' piece of meat, it jumped into the water to procure the reflection, and lost its true meat. She would get involved in innumerable jobs as a volunteer – something she also regretted – with two main purposes: to hide her aggression by giving the impression, to herself and others, that she was a 'very good girl', and also, to make herself important as a form of compensation for her own oedipal feelings of insignificance. However, nothing was enough, because whatever position she obtained, it automatically became unimportant by the simple fact that she had obtained it. Like Tantalus' punishment,[44] it was an 'insignificance' in search of a 'significance' that always receded and was never reached, because once she felt she had found it, it automatically became 'insignificant'.

Another central reason for the failure of this longing for the lost object results from the fact that the need to secure its presence is always a matter from the past, an emotional and historical memory that can never be achieved because its search would always be out of time. It is something that the adult or the non-traumatised state in us knows well, but, because there is usually no communication between the non-traumatised and the traumatised states, the issue will never be properly dealt with. Obviously, the only escape from this trap would be to relinquish any form of desire towards the 'lost object'; a mechanism advocated by Oriental philosophy such as Zen Buddhism, where any form of 'attachment' to the original objects, as well as compulsive 'desires', are systematically forsaken using self-restraint.

---

44 Tantalus, a figure from Greek mythology, was famously punished by being made to stand for eternity in a pool of water, with a fruit tree over his head. Whenever he reached for the fruit, the branch would rise above his reach; whenever thirst compelled him to drink, the water drained away from his cupped hand.

VENGEFUL HOPE VS. RENUNCIATION HOPE

The main purpose of life is to reach an inner state of *well-being* or inner peace, to free the mind from any disturbing element and to always remain on the alert for any kind of toxic thinking. As far as I know, there are mainly two instruments widely used for that purpose: meditation, and psychoanalysis, including psychoanalytic psychotherapy. The main difference between the two is that, in meditation, all forms of thinking are avoided, while, in psychoanalysis, noxious and creative thinking are differentiated and only the deleterious are dodged. I refer to 'toxic thinking' as thoughts related to pre-conceptual traumas (primary lost objects), usually in the form of childhood emotions that repeat compulsively. The main purpose of psychoanalysis would be to help the non-traumatised state to 'contain' the traumatised through recognition of the profile of the pre-conceptual trauma or beta elements – using Bion's language – with the use of cognitive thinking and common sense or, following Bion again, digesting beta elements and changing them into alpha, with the use of cognitive processes or 'alpha function' (Bion, 1967; López-Corvo, 2003, 2014). This ongoing and continuous operation would strengthen one's capacity to rise above toxic thinking by relinquishing the desire or longing for the loss of primary objects. It would subdue the compulsive use of 'vengeful hope', a dynamic that will always amount to unconscious guilt, continuous mental pain and perilous physical ailments, and, even more, premature death. It is not with ease that the traumatised state gives up unconscious mental structures, which have dominated the mind for such a long time that it has built up a strong 'resistance' to any possibility of mental growth. We ought to use 'binocular vision', as Bion often recommended; in other words, to become 'cross eyed', with one eye focused on outside reality and the other toward the intra-psychic – to the pre-conceptual trauma and the interaction between the traumatised and the non-traumatised states – to 'race above' or to 'ride our genes', to stay put and remain in the present, avoiding the past that does not exist, and also never going into the future that is not here yet.

Chapter VIII
EXCESS OF MOTHER AND ABSENCE OF FATHER, LONELINESS AND THE PHANTASY OF THE "FECAL PHALLUS"

A 'Freedom Drive'

Both parents are absolutely indispensable for the mental upbringing of children. The role of the mother is close to biology, to Nature, while the father is more related to social aspects: this is why the Greeks used the earth (Gaia) to represent the mother, and the heavens (Uranus) as well as the time (Kronos) to represent the father. As I have stated in the previous chapter, the mother provides *life* and *unconditional love*, while the father is responsible for *hope* and *independence*. I think there is a sort of 'freedom drive' which can be discerned from the manner of how Nature performs, always moving from dependency towards autonomy. We are created within our mother's entrails and remain as such for nine months, as if we were another of her internal organs. Birth arrives and we achieve the biological status of being 'another' individual (*undivided*), absolutely different from our parents, but only from a biological dimension because, from a psychological vertex, we remain dependent for many years. The continuous process of complex 'bio-psycho-social' maturation and symbolisation (motion, speech, conceptualisation, mental growth, and so on) relentlessly moves us towards further states of autonomy and freedom. Since it is difficult for children to create by themselves a mental space that helps them escape from the attraction of the maternal natural symbiosis, the father will usually function as such a force, capable of neutralising the mother's gravitational pull. This is why there is the expression that the 'phallus introduces the symbol', where the 'symbol' means the successive process of introjection, identification and representations that will continuously amount to further autonomic behaviour, or, in other words: '*freedom*'. Great changes, ontogenetic as well as phylogenetic, are a product of symbolisation, like for instance the appearance of language, representing the exchange of the 'absence of a thing', for a particular sound or sign, socially supported by a common-sense agreement. I have previously stated that money

> ...is another good example, since we no longer need currency to embody its own value, as old gold coins did in the past, or to bring animals or things for trading, we use plastic cards or e-trades instead, which we exchange freely, solely on the basis of trust induced by symbolization and common knowledge. *Symbols* maintain a close and meaningful tie to the objects they represent, while *signs* [language] keep a fortuitous attachment to them. It would be similar to the distinction between blood or natural family ties and legal ones, respectively. Often the relationship between the symbol and the signified object appears hazy, veiled by metaphors and requires a keen eye in order to reveal the hidden meaning; however, in art as well as in poetry for example, such awkwardness and vagueness in the affiliation, displays beauty and elegance. (López-Corvo, 2014, p. 70)

Symbolisation as well as mental growth, which engines the non-traumatised state, constitutes an imperative and regular resource towards natural freedom in every human being. Pre-conceptual traumas, on the other hand, which structure the 'traumatised state' act as a decisive disturbing element that interferes with the normal process of maturation induced by the progressive 'freedom drive' by means of 'compulsive repetition' of those primitive and ubiquitous traumatic historical events from early childhood.

Meltzer (1992) referred to the metaphorical spaces or claustrum inside the mother's body where individuals may remain mentally 'confined'. He described three of them: i) head/breast, ii) genital and iii) maternal rectum. I believe, however, that from a clinical point of view there is always a combination of all of these possibilities with predominance of one claustrum over the other. The first claustrum can be represented by the attitude or behaviour present in a person or a culture often associated with

> ...richness, at first concrete and related to urgent need of nourishment, becomes diversified in its nuances: generosity, receptiveness, aesthetic reciprocity; [If seen from inside]... generosity becomes quid pro quo, receptiveness becomes inveiglement, reciprocity becomes collusion, understanding becomes penetration of secrets, knowledge becomes information, symbol formation becomes metonymy, art becomes fashion. [Meltzer, 1992, pp. 72, 73]

The head/breast, as a form of interaction, is different from the genital and the rectum, in the sense that someone trapped in the former could become a resourceful writer or a successful entrepreneur. In my own case, both my mother and grandmother were school teachers and compulsive readers. I learned to read very early, before attending school, thanks to my grandmothers' patience and dedication, and, like them, I also became a compulsive reader and developed a desire to write. I remember that, in my adolescence, I experienced a deep sense of inner peace every time I opened a dictionary or an encyclopaedia, an experience I did not then consider and did not provide a meaning to until I read Meltzer's concept of 'claustrum'.

The second space, or genital claustrum related to sexual perversions, has been defined by Meltzer as having the following characteristics:

> The inmates of this space are more obviously disturbed and turbulent…they live in a space dominated by a primitive priapic religion…seen from the interior is Mardi Gras…for the essence of this interior view is that the entry of the father's phallus is celebrated and enjoyed voluptuously by all the babies, while the mother calmly receives this homage. [Ibid, pp. 88, 89]

In the maternal rectum,

> …we are essentially in the world of addiction, where the individual has consigned his survival to the mercy of a malignant object [Ibid, p. 92].

A significant feature present in this last claustrum is the idealisation of faeces, where the child represents the mother's phantasy of an envious and revengeful internal object, depicted by the symbolism of a 'faecal penis' or what we could consider as an '*empty plenitude*'. Remembering Freud's well-known statement of 'penis = child = faeces', the oedipal 'child-faecal-penis' is eternally hidden in his mother's rectum where he will remain motionless as a dead object. I have previously stated the following:

EXCESS OF MOTHER AND ABSENCE OF FATHER

The figure of the 'child-faecal-penis' represents a crucial mechanism or extreme form of ambivalence, used by some mothers towards their children, usually boys, and constitutes a condensation of two opposite desires: i) the mother's need to resolve her own castration anxiety by providing herself with the phantasy of her child as an imaginary penis; ii) and at the same time, to enviously attack (self-envy) this needed penis by rendering it useless and degrading it to faeces, often related to Freud's concept of the 'cloacae theory' or zonal confusion between the vagina and the anus, as well as revenge towards the oedipal father. [Also, as a way to avoid incest with the chosen boy] In other words, the future addict – usually marijuana dependent – identifies himself with his mother's desire by becoming her useless 'faecal-phallus'. [López-Corvo, 1993, p. 59]

And also:

Faeces [or drugs in addictions] are experienced not only as babies who live inside the anus, but also as food to feed them. The mother could also be preserved inside the baby's anus in the form of mother-breast-faeces-baby, withheld, controlled, or expelled with omnipotence at their wish. [Ibid]

Some characteristics present in these patients appear to be universal, beyond the limitations imposed by culture, and I have observed them in my analytical practice in Latin America (Venezuela) as well as in North America (Canada and USA); or beyond time, as we will see further on in the case of Baudelaire, born in 1821. They are usually adolescents or very young adults, most of them males, chronic abusers of marijuana, colloquially nicknamed 'potheads', school dropouts, unemployed, with little ambition, living with their parents and financially dependent on them. *They are always the result of a universal equation: an excess of motherhood and an emotionally or physically absent father.* Clinically, these patients experience dissociated states, displaying fantasies of grandeur that are never accomplished, where fantasy is confused with reality, and could be summarised as: 'how to do everything in order to end up doing nothing', a condition I have previously referred to as 'Sisyphus complex'.[45] I recall the case of a patient, a heavy user of marihuana, a singer and composer, who once wrote a song he named 'the gonorrhoea', that was so vulgar that the place where he worked did not allow him to sing it! In other words, just as the total presence of a mother is absolutely indispensable for a child to achieve a psychological state of well being, there is also the danger of the child being retained by the mother – 'in the mother's anal claustrum',[46] Meltzer (1992) – beyond the utterly indispensable time required by the youngster to evolve normally. The father, on the other hand, is absolutely essential for a child to achieve a sense of psychological freedom, because men, due to their own biological endowment, usually do not possess a mental space capable of inducing a sense of withholding like women do.

The 'Faecal Phallus'

In mothers with borderline structure there is sometimes a significant ambivalence that contains at once dialectical and contradictory emotions, like *denigration* and *idealisation* of the phallus, a paradox that will result in the creation of the fantasy of the 'faecal phallus', in which she makes the child her unconscious phallus by denigrating and castrating him. Mothers who follow this pattern

---

[45] See "Sisyphus's myth" in López-Corvo 2014.
[46] See: Chapter VI.

will lack the capacity to establish a cooperative relationship with a man, and will often choose partners whom they could disparage for being 'too passive', 'too dependent', 'too busy', a womaniser, or rather absent; often resulting in divorce and becoming 'single mothers'. They could obliterate, in this way, the possibility of the child having a father, who could eventually break the mother's narcissistic symbiosis and provide the child with a sense of freedom, hope and independence, instead of remaining for ever the mother's unconscious solution for her 'narcissistic absence' or absence of a penis. When this takes place and the child is unconsciously chosen by the mother to become the solution for her castration anxiety, this child will eventually become, through a process of identification, the mother's faecal phallus, or following Meltzer's remark (1992) a child from the 'anal claustrum'.

This is a mechanism always present in drug addiction; in those patients often referred to as 'potheads', or someone who chronically abuses marijuana. This drug is capable of destroying volition, concentration and memory, resulting at the end in self-castration and total emotional dependency, or, in other words, a 'faecal phallus'. I remember the case of the young man, unable to go beyond the first year of psychology at the university, who presented as a chronic user of marijuana and whose mother, who was a judge, had decided to provide him with the drug he needed in order to – according to her – 'protect him from the danger of buying drugs in the street'! Insight into the cause of marijuana addiction in young men can perhaps be gleaned by the following case of a patient in analysis, which I had previously published in 2014:

> A 50-year-old widow, the mother of an adolescent who presented with chronic dependency on marijuana and was hospitalized abroad due to his addiction, consulted me with the purpose of discussing her son's troubles and to provide her

with assistance once her son was back in the country. Once he came back, he demanded, as a form of contract, that not only should he receive help, but that his mother should do it as well. I will now review two sessions that took place around one year after the beginning of her analysis. By this time, we were working on her aversion to silence as a reaction to separation and weaning anxiety from an internal, needy, and fragile element, terribly envious about the omnipotent penis-breast projected through the transference, which she ambivalently, also attacked. She often demanded that I say something, just anything to confirm my presence, then immediately, rejected everything I interpreted, something that produced countertransference feelings of being trapped, paralyzed and impotent. At the beginning of the session she stated that her son had become angry when she had poured in his meal, without asking, the same sauce she was eating. 'He didn't like it that I wanted him to have the same taste that I did.' Then she said that her sister had accused her of being ambitious, something she did not like because she felt it was not true, or like me (analyst) also, who had accused her of being envious and distrustful. She gave her sister equal partnership in her business, though she only contributed 30% of the capital. When they could no longer get along together, she 'fired' her, but paid her everything she demanded, '...So, how could she say that I am ambitious?... Anyway... Could you look it up in the dictionary?...You are not going to look for anything...And you are not even going to answer?' After a short silence, which I judged as a test, I said that she did not like the fact that we did not have the same taste, and that I did not do exactly as she wanted. She would like for me to become her partner so she could fire me afterwards. She then became very upset and stated that she understood nothing. I felt she was incapable of freeing herself from the 'narcissistic weight' of the *other*. She resisted with terror anything she conceived as 'heterogeneous', as different, like the outside space, the unlikeness; it was like a true form of 'heterophobia', or fear of 'otherness'. It was essential to capture and withhold the object in order to expel it afterwards at her own urge. She was the eldest of three girls, and very early together with her mother, were all abandoned by her father once he left the country due to political reasons. She grew up with a deep sense of responsibility for her two younger sisters and her frightened, insecure and economically dependent mother. This feeling, together with an aggressive sibling rivalry, induced in her the need to identify with the absent father as a form of denying the painful lost. At a given moment, she revealed with great difficulty and anxiety, a masturbatory phantasy where she felt in possession of an artificial penis. At the next session, she talked about her brother-in-law, and of his need to take sleeping pills, and asked if I could give her a prescription. 'He is so...skinny, so insignificant, always depressed. He was the eldest of three brothers, was never wanted by his mother and was born with a fractured arm. When his mother died they found him huddled in his apartment, sleeping on a mattress on the floor, with a candle illuminating his own picture when he was a baby, several Teddy bears and dolls scattered around, plates, clothes throughout the garden. It was horrible...(pause)...F (her own son) is travelling to the USA and he wished to take his girlfriend with him, and I said it was unnecessary to take her because he is going there to work, and I don't know what is he going to do there with her.' At that moment, she lifted her head off the couch and said jokingly: 'You should put something on the pillow so I don't get contaminated from other patients.' Then I said to her, that she wished to be the only child, without other 'couch' sisters, or perhaps she wanted to be different from her own sisters, perhaps to be a boy, although she was becoming more aware, with great sadness and horror, that she was not a boy. She did not wish to be such an 'insignificant' boy resembling her brother-in-law, who like her, was born with a fractured arm-penis, with a fabricated penis, a lie. It was difficult for her to imagine, or possibly filled her with envy to think, that there were other men who received a real penis and wished to use it, like her son F with his girlfriend. [López-Corvo, 2014].

Baudelaire and the Faecal Phallus

Charles Pierre Baudelaire (1821–1867) presents an important case to consider, not only because he was a heavy user of illegal drugs, but also because he was born 150 years prior to the appearance of what was referred to as 'the drug culture' which emerged around the seventies in the last century. However, the most significant aspect to reflect on in his own history is the existence – beyond time and culture – of the equation I have often observed in drug dependent youth, of an *excessive mother* and an *absent father*. Baudelaire died of syphilis – comparable to AIDS of the present time – at the age of forty-six, extremely poor and completely unknown, after some publications during his life time, which did not receive the true merit that his literary geniality as a poet deserved. The dissolute form of life he engaged in during his university years led to his expulsion, accused of pederasty, a situation that had three main consequences: i) the impossibility of finishing his studies of law; ii) throwing himself wholeheartedly into the debauchery of life in the Latin Quarter, where he contracted syphilis; iii) being forced by his parents to travel to India in order to break him from his lifestyle – a trip he failed to finish because he only went as far as Mauritius; however, the trip had a significant influence on his ingenuity as a poet.

Throughout his tempestuous existence, Baudelaire exhibited a significant masochism, something often present in drug addicted patients, related to extreme guilt and emotional confusions. These patients, usually young adults, resort to attacking their internal parents – as a form of revenge – by refusing to 'give them the "nice child" they think their internal parents wished for them to be', an action that fills them with guilt and, as a consequence, triggers the need to punish themselves. It is a mechanism I have previously referred to as 'self-envy' (López-Corvo, 1992, 1995, 1997). In a letter written in 1860 to a friend, Charles Baudelaire said:

> "I have been taken for a pederast by a policeman (serves me right!), [and] It was I who spread the story and people believed me!"

And Sartre (1950), his biographer, added:

> ...He was probably the source of the unfounded perfidious rumors reported... that he had been expelled from the *Licee Louis-le-Grand* for homosexuality. But he not only attributed vices to himself; he went so far as to make himself look ridiculous. [p. 87]

And also:

> We might even say that Baudelaire's whole life was a punishment. I cannot discover in it an accident or any of those misfortunes which can be described as underserved or unexpected. There was nothing down to his syphilis which he did not bring on almost of his own accord. At any rate, he

knowingly ran the risk of syphilis as a young man because he said that he was tempted by the most squalid prostitutes. Filth, physical wretchedness, illness and the poorhouse were the things that attracted him and the things he liked in Sarah *l'affreuse Juive*.[47] [Ibid, p.p. 86–88]

Charles Pierre Baudelaire's father, François Baudelaire, an older civil servant and amateur artist, was forty-five years older than his mother and died in 1827, when Charles was only seven year old. His mother, Caroline, who became an orphan from the age of seven and was raised by a friend of the family, was twenty-seven years old when Charles was born. She became extremely attached to him, possibly as a compensation for two significant facts present in her own history: the loneliness she might have experienced as an orphaned child,[48] and the age and generational difference that existed between her and her husband. It is quite possible that Charles became a toy for Caroline, a 'teddy bear', to whom she attached herself as a compensation for the loneliness resulting from such an uneven union to a man old enough to be her father. Losing her husband could have represented for Caroline a situation similar to the loss of her father when she was a child, which could have left her desolated once more. She was remarried to Lieutenant Colonel Jacques Aupick – a senator who later became a French ambassador – just one year after Charles' father had died. Shortly after this marriage, Charles was sent to a boarding school, possibly as a demand

---

47 *'The horrible Jew woman.'*
48 I have observed a similar situation in the life of Ernesto 'Che' Guevara, whose mother became an orphan when she was a child, and, after having Ernesto, he became for her the only blood related human being, inducing her to become so attached to him that she emotionally suffocated him to the point that he developed asthma. (See: Perez-Morazzani & López-Corvo, 2017.)

from the new husband. This decision became the core of Charles' 'pre-conceptual trauma', which marked him for life due to the immense contrast existing between two critical moments in his life: i) how, prior to her second marriage, his mother gave herself completely to his care; ii) how lonely, desecrated, and betrayed he must have felt after being sent away at the tender age of eight, because someone else had taken his place in his mother's heart. In May 1861 he wrote to his mother a sentiment he had often expressed before:

> During my childhood, there was a period when I loved you passionately. Listen and don't be afraid to read on. I have never said so much about it to you before...I was always living in you; you belonged to me alone. You were at once an idol and a friend. [Ibid, p.p. 60–61]

And also:

> ...when one has a son like me – 'like me' was understood – one doesn't remarry." [Ibid, p. 17]

Surrounded by every care and comfort before he was sent away, he did not yet realise that he existed as a separate person, but felt that he was united body and soul to his mother in a primitive mystical relationship; a feeling that changed drastically to total disappointment, once his mother got married and he was sent away to a boarding school, producing the unconscious and paradoxical feelings of 'all and nothing' or the *empty plenitude*; an ambivalence he later described as follows:

> When I was only a child I felt in my heart two contradictory sentiments, the horror of life and the ecstasy of life. [Ibid, p. 76]

Later in his life, not only did he wish to become his mother's appendix, her phallus, but an indecent appendix, undesirable, low, dirty and illegal, as he once stated:

> When I've aroused universal horror and disgust, I shall have conquered solitude. [Ibid, p. 87]

In Baudelaire, we could clearly observe the symbolical imbroglio I have previously referred as the 'fecal phallus', representing a narcissistic condition where addicts unconsciously try to fulfil the mother's phallic envy, or a kind of appendix, a fantasy we could guess in Baudelaire's verse:

> *J'ausse aime vivre d'une jeune geante, Comme aux pieds d'une reine un chat voluptueux.*"[49]

The disequilibrium we always find in addiction, between an excess of motherhood and a lack of fatherhood, played a significant part in Baudelaire's upbringing. In a letter he wrote to his mother in later life, he referred to this matter:

> I am ill, ill. I have an execrable temperament because of my parents. I ramble because of them. Here you have what means to be the son of a twenty-seven year old mother and of a seventy-two father. A disproportionate union, pathological, senile. Think about it: forty-five years of difference…Ask

---

49 *'I would like to live from a young giant, As a voluptuous cat at the feet of a queen.'*

> your teacher about what does he thinks of the haphazard product of such a coupling. [Ibid, p. 159]

The 'fecal phallus' represents the ambivalence an adolescent will display as a response to his mother's own ambivalence towards men; she may wish to have a penis like a man, but envies and resents men for not being able to fulfil herself this desire. The fact that she remarried an 'absent man' may have represented her desire to debase men, and neutralise a father's capacity to break the mother's narcissistic symbiosis to her child. Following his mother's ambivalence of needing a boy to fulfil her narcissistic absence, while at the same time denigrating men, could induce the adolescent to unconsciously seek to provide her with a loving child who was equally a total failure. However, there is also the possibility that the adolescent resents his mother's need for him to become her 'eternal child', to give up his biological wish to move ahead towards independence and autonomy, and eventually to accomplish his own ambitions. It is interesting to observe that in the majority of cases these boys are addicted to the chronic use of marihuana ('pot-heads'), whose main effect on the mind is the destruction of 'concentration and memory', two functions categorically crucial in the acquisition of knowledge and fundamental to the process of attaining autonomy and independence. Thus deprived of their thinking capacity or 'alpha function', they are unable to 'contain' their traumatised state.

Chapter IX
LONELINESS, FEELING OF 'NON-EXISTENCE', AND THE NEED OF A 'RESCUER'

> 'Ubi nihil vales, ibi nihil velis'
> *(Where you are worth nothing, you should want nothing)*
> — Arnold Geulincx
> (1624 –1669)

Childhood loneliness and the human need for a 'Rescuer'

Several years ago, when my oldest son was five, I decided to revive my own childhood experiences of slight-of-hand magic. My son was very impressed, and jumped for joy whenever I performed a new trick. However, when I decided at one point to reveal to him the true nature of the trick, I was astounded to find my son throw himself on the floor, crying and dejected. It took some time before I comprehended that he was not interested whatsoever in understanding the hidden mechanism of the tricks, or learning anything about prestidigitation. His main enjoyment relied in thinking that his father had the unbelievable power to make things appear and disappear, that he was mighty and omnipotent. He was terrified by the threat of finding out that everything could have been just a lie.

I have found a similar reaction in British buccaneer Francis Drake's account of his expedition to the West Coast of the United States in 1579. He landed in the area now known as 'Point Reyes' and 'Drake Bay' in California. There he met the Miwok Indians and the following comments were chronicled:

> Drake distributed shirts and linen cloth, entreating them [the Indians] to cover their nakedness, and made a display of eating and drinking to show that he and his men were not gods [as the Indians believed them to be] but more mortals like themselves. After exchanging gifts, the Indians return to their village, about three-quarters of a mile distant, where 'a kind of most lamentable weeping and crying out' was heard, 'the women especially extending their voices in a most miserable and doleful manner of shrieking…as if they have been desperate, used unnatural violence against themselves, crying and shrieking pitifully, tearing their flesh with their nails…' [Bawlf, 2003, pp. 317–318]

Like my son, I gather, they felt so lonely and disillusioned to find out that the British were not true gods who could have saved and protected them, but were instead just plain helpless mortals liked themselves.

Whenever the individual perceives the 'presence' of a 'possible rescuer', they automatically experience a sense of consolation or solace, or the opposite – hopelessness and depression – when they fail, for example, a patient raised by nannies always sensed a powerful feeling of comfort whenever a babysitter was present. Another patient, after some years in analysis, decided to search for his childhood nanny; at the moment he heard her voice on the telephone, he unexpectedly experienced the feeling of 'being safe'. A forty-three year old woman who, at around the age of six, lived several months with her grandparents, experienced a sensation of 'inner peace' whenever she caught the particular smell of her grandfather's pipe tobacco, something she still feels whenever she comes into contact with that smell. I observe such peace in myself whenever I open a dictionary or an encyclopedia, possibly because my mother and grandmother were both school teachers. Another patient described similar feelings of comfort whenever he was cooking. His mother, of Italian extraction, and who was a wonderful cook, fervently protected him as a child from a punitive and aggressive father.

As I have frequently said in this book, 'loneliness' is always at the core of the 'pre-conceptual trauma', for the simple reason that children are biologically restricted to only one source of security and protection, the one provided by their parents' safekeeping. At the moment the parents act impatiently and irately to any 'wrong-doing', the child, has nobody to turn to for protection, an attitude that epitomes the conceptualisation of complete abandonment, destitution and total loneliness. Additionally, before the age of six or seven, children are unable to enduringly sustain in their mind the image of a person once that person has disappeared from their sight, making *separations*, even short ones, catastrophic events, because children experience the absent person – the mother mostly – as if they were dead, and, even worse, as if they have killed them with their own anger. It is this dynamic that is often behind children's anxiety, often described as 'school phobia', meaning that the main conflict is not at the school, but within the child's mind. In my practice, I have suggested a 'golden rule' for parents – something they usually do not wish to hear! – I recommend that they never separate, unless they really have to, more than one day per year of the child's age, and to always discuss and explain to their children ahead of time all the details of their departure and homecoming.

THE NEED OF A 'RESCUER'

I apologise for being so repetitive, but I cannot put too fine a point on the fact that there is always, in all human beings, a continuous dialectic struggle between the 'traumatised' and the 'non-traumatised states', wherein the 'traumatised state' is always structured following 'confused childhood emotions', which remain unconscious, representing essentials that Bion has addressed as 'beta elements'. The 'non-traumatised', on the other hand, signifies the cognitive progression from childhood to adulthood and corresponds to Bion's 'alpha world', which contains the 'alpha function' capable of digesting 'beta elements' and changing them into 'alpha, or thoughts good for thinking'. When the 'adult part' or 'non-traumatised state' is 'contained' by the child part or 'traumatised state', childlike feelings of confused emotions such as desperation, loneliness, helplessness, hopelessness, depression, anxiety, and so on, will take over and control the mind. There are emotions resulting from pre-conceptual traumas that will unconsciously take over the adult's mind, making feelings already manufactured during childhood – mostly of loneliness and helplessness – to 'contain' the mind and to be re-experienced again, ignoring they origin, but believing they were facts that resulted from something taking place at the present time. The assault made by the traumatised state over the thinking mind via mechanisms of 'self-envy', together with the silence and lack of help from the *paralysed* non-traumatised state,[50] will always produce an inner feeling of being 'devoid of inner help', and, as a consequence, having to resort to the need to search for outside help from idealised, omnipotent and magic rescuers, like religion, for instance. I will expand on this subject further on.

---

50 For clarification of this aspect, see the end of Chapter I.

Feeling of non-existence and the source of 'Meaning'

We can often find adults who lack a sense of being alive, who do not have a point of view, a perspective from where they could witness their inner and outer world, a condition common among adolescents who often are not able to discriminate between themselves and others, who feel 'altered'[51] and lack a sense of 'selfness'. Usually the emotion behind this attitude is fear, which comes directly from limitations experienced in childhood, from their particular pre-conceptual trauma that afterwards, in adulthood, shapes the structure of the 'traumatised state'.

To lack a sense of being alive is usually the consequence of how adults were treated by their parents when children, whether they were provided or not with 'meaning' by their caregivers. I have already reflected on this aspect in the Preface and in Chapter I, where I stated that this sense of 'non-existence' is present in adults who, as children, were not considered or treated with the respect one would afford an important and existing individual. Instead, they were ignored or sidestepped as if they were entirely insignificant. In Accordance with the pre-conceptual trauma, an inner sense of 'meaning' is always provided by the caregivers: if it is provided, it will result in the individual producing their own 'meaning', a source Bion described as 'narcissistic', but when it is not provided, 'meaning' will always be solicited from the other; it will then be 'social-istic' (Bion, 1965, p. 81). To use a simile, narcissistic 'meaning' could be comparable to how the value of a 'gold

---

51 The word 'altered' originates from the Latin 'alter' which means 'other', denoting something like: 'to be changed by the inner presence of the Other', or we might say: '*othered*'. When the alteration is even greater, we might use 'disturbed', which also originates from the Latin '*turba*', meaning a 'distressed crowd' or to feel distressed not by one, but by many.

coin' is implicit in the coin itself; while social-istic meaning is like a dollar bill, whose value lies only in its association to other structures, such as banks. For narcissistic 'meaning' to exist in the non-traumatised state, the individual need simply exist 'in their own truth', which is absolutely personal and 'unique'. They do not need a thinker in order to be; they just are, provided with an intrinsic meaning based on their own truth. Social-istic 'meaning', on the other hand, which structures the traumatised state, depends entirely on external influences such as the opinions and reactions of people around; meaning can only exist in relation to others and not to themselves.

'Meaning' can also be cultural and geographically determined, something I have observed often in patients from Asian cultures, where men exercise total control over women and treat them like commodities, as if they were not alive, without any kind of independence or a true sense of selfness. These women go on to treat their children in the same manner. A high prevalence of criminality could also be an expression of lacking a sense of being alive,[52] like what happens with suicide terrorism for instance. About this matter, Bion (1970) said the following:

> Non-existence, immediately becomes an object that is immensely hostile, and filled with murderous envy towards

---

[52] Once there was an invasion of tiny ants in my house, not larger than a millimeter. As I was eating on the pantry table, the ants were passing by in the junction between the edge of the table and the wall. I killed one of them and then observed that all the others that were coming behind, acting estranged. Just at the exact place where I 'murdered' the ant, they wiggled in circles, as in despair, then either continued their way or turned back. As they met others that were coming, they 'chatted' for a second and 'convinced' them to return. I came away with the insight that any living being that has an awareness of death deserves respect, regardless of how meaningless they might appear! If the tiger were aware of the suffering of the gazelle, it would starve to death!

the quality of function of 'existence', wherever it is to be found. [p. 19–21]

These feelings would be personified by a 'non-existent' person,

> ...whose hatred and envy is such, that "it" is determined to remove and destroy every scrap of "existence" from any object which might be considered to "have" any existence to remove. Such a non-existent object, can be terrifying that its "existence" is denied leaving only the "place where it was" [Bion, 1965, p. 111]

This envy from a 'non-existence' component could also be directed to inner 'existing' elements within the same individual, following dynamics I have previously referred to as 'self-envy', or 'envy between internal parts'. (López-Corvo, 1992, 1995, 1999, 2003). In the transference of these patients, there is often a tendency towards 'negative therapeutic reaction', where the interpretation is thought to be a form of criticism or prejudicial confrontation, reproducing the *dialectical* interaction that once took place between the child – now symbolised by internalised ego part-objects – and the parents, signified by superego internal part-objects, often projected in the therapist as a transference. It is a dynamic that usually reproduces children's envy towards their parents' own alpha function or capacity to reason, an envy that is then internalised and replicated between internal part-objects as a form of self-envy, and then repeated in the transference, as an envious attack towards the analyst's alpha function. In any dialogue or discussion between two individuals, there are at least three elements involved: the two *individuals* plus the *subject* of discussion. If we choose between two extreme forms of deliberation, like *consensual* or *confrontational*, the main difference between these two will depend on the relevance given to either the *individuals* or to the *subject* of the argument. In the consensual discussion, the *subject* is always more germane than the *individuals*, whereas in the confrontational it will be the opposite, meaning the *individuals* prevail over the *subject*. What clouds the *subject* and makes the difference between the two discussants more significant is always the presence of the envy once experienced as children towards the adult parents' capacity to reason, which is now experienced as self-envy and mutually projected to each other by the *confrontational* discussants. It is 'self-envy', because the main purpose of the argument when the subject of discussion is dismissed is to attack in each other the capacity to reason logically, or what Bion refers to as 'alpha function', repeating what was once equally experienced towards the parents' reasoning.

Feelings of non-existence will always induce the endless argumentative interaction between the master and the slave.[53] Loneliness is always a consequence of the interaction between me and myself and never between me and the other. It is a psychological matter, and never a sociological substance, or, to use Bion's terminology, it is 'narcissistic' and not 'social-istic'. People who feel lonely could live surrounded by a crowd and still feel lonely, while someone who does not feel lonely could live in isolation and not feel lonely. The true conflict is more the consequence of inner feelings of non-existence related to the traumatised state.

Loneliness or Aloneness

In summary, there are two important emotional states that appear very similar, although they are very different. I am referring to *loneliness* and *aloneness*. The first is present in children who, being biologically and emotionally dependent, lack the ability of rescue

---

53 I believe that this form of dialectical interaction is magnificently expressed by Beckett in the characters of Pozzo and Lucky in "Waiting for Godot".

themselves. It is also present in the 'traumatised state' and will predominate in any given individual's mind, whenever this state *contains* the 'non-traumatised', inducing feelings of despair, depression, and even suicide. The opposite, when the 'non-traumatised' *contains* the 'traumatised state', there could be experienced a sense of 'aloneness', different from 'loneliness' and similar to what Heidegger has described as 'Dasein', or *the paradox of living in relationship to the world and to other humans, while at the same time being in the predicament or remaining ultimately alone but in relation to oneself.* Being in 'relation to oneself', like having 'narcissistic meaning', represents the adult or 'non-traumatised' element in us, who is capable of looking after oneself, with the same, or perhaps better, skill that someone else could, or even superior to what our parents did in their turn. The 'traumatised state' is ruled by 'pathological narcissism', where 'living' and 'meaning' are at all times experienced in *relation to the 'Other'*, and in a complete confusion of time and space; like being trapped in a total unconscious incapacity to discriminate the present from the past (such as the transference) or between internal and external realities (like in projective and introjective identifications). This confusion of *time* and *space* always induces the need to continuously look for an *outside* 'rescuer', to provide meaning and hope, often representing our projected parent's imago, instead of resorting to our own capacity to rescue our self, by the adult that, with time, we have now become. The 'non-traumatised' state is ruled by 'normal narcissism', or the capacity of becoming our best friend and only 'rescuer'; or, in simple terms, to follow Obermann's statement: 'For the universe I might be nobody, but for myself, I am everything.'[54] Or what Seneca wrote in Letter 6 to Lucilius: *'What progress, you ask, have I made? I have begun to be a friend to*

---

54 Cited by Unamuno, 1954; p. 47.

myself. That was indeed a great benefit; such a person can never be lonely. You may be sure that such a man is a friend to all mankind.'[55]

The 'Rescuer'

I often think that Heidegger's definition of 'Dasein' is too generous when describing humans as being 'full of existence', although absolutely forsaken. I think the situation is much more sombre, like being a *'speck of nothingness, completely surrounded by a dark, thick, and impenetrable mystery'*. I also believe that there is a general and intuitive grasp of such a condition, inducing as a consequence a sense of total desertion; more obvious at an older age than in the younger generations. As a defence, this 'sense of desertion' induces a need for a continuous search for the presence of a saviour or 'rescuer'.

The phenomenology of the rescuer is universal, but differs according to historical progression and geographical differences. Common rescuers are God, religion, saints, religious personalities, oracles, soothsayers, babies, dead persons, medical doctors, money, power, and so on. In the past, families made sure one of their children followed a religious organisation in order to secure an ambassador for the 'Kingdom of Heaven', in the manner of procuring someone who could provide a place near God, and 'save' their souls.

Ferenczi (1949) had previously referred to the 'wise baby' in these terms:

> I wish to remind you of the typical 'dream of the wise baby' described by me several years ago in which a newly-born

---

[55] Wikisource: 'Moral letters to Lucilius'. Internet: en.wikisource.org/wiki/Moral_letters_to_Lucilius/Letter_6

child or infant begins to talk, in fact teaches wisdom to the entire family. The fear of the uninhibited, almost mad adult changes the child, so to speak, into a psychiatrist and, in order to become one and to defend himself against dangers coming from people without self-control, he must know how to identify himself completely with them. Indeed, it is unbelievable how much we can still learn from our wise children, the neurotics. [p. 228]

The 'Rescuer' and Bion's 'Basic Assumptions'

An important aspect of this external search for a 'rescuer' – when the 'traumatised state' contains and rules the mind – is that, besides the key feelings of helplessness and loneliness that often induce the need for the outside search, there are also other emotions that could determine the particular characteristics of the specific 'rescuer' the person is attempting to procure. These characteristics, I believe, follow outlines based on mechanisms Bion has described in group dynamics, as 'basic assumptions',[56] such as '*dependence*', '*pairing*' and '*flight-fight*'. I think that the choice of the specific 'basic assumption' will be made contingent to the predominant emotions present in the traumatised state, such as oral needs, guilt, and depression in 'dependence'; vengeful hope in 'pairing'; and anger, hate, and envy in 'flight-fight'. We could find illustrations about the kind of 'rescuer' that has been used, following the 'basic assumptions', although in reality there might be at the same time a combination of more than one

---

56 Bion uses 'basic assumptions' (ba) to represent emotional complications, which appear at a given moment in a rather automatic, involuntarily and unavoidable manner within a working group (W), changing its direction and determining how it will function subsequently. He described three kinds of ba: 'dependence', 'pairing' and 'fight-flight'. See Bion (1948); López-Corvo (2003).

assumption. Religion, God, doctors, dead people, mentors and so on represent a form of 'dependence'; while babies, who are baptised using heroes' names, might reflect 'pairing'; and identification with powerful and angry fathers, following Ana Freud's description of 'identification with the aggressor', could point out to the fight in 'flight-fight' assumption; while 'flight' could be perhaps observed in the tendency towards a 'regressive scape', like suicide or Alzheimer, for instance. The superego can also be a form of rescuer by means of masochism, like the need for self-punishment in order to reduce guilt and anxiety and to be rescued by means of commiseration, a mechanism usually observed in the transference-countertransference interaction, in masochistic patients who resort to a continuous form of exaggerated self-flagellation in order to elicit the countertransference need to openly intervene, in order to liberate them from their self-attack.

The main issue surrounding any form of rescuer is that eventually all of them fail, inducing the need for an endless and continuous search for a rescuer. The truth is that there is no rescuer, because all existing human beings are exactly in the 'same boat' – regardless of any mundane benefit they could have managed to achieved – and there is not any other form of productive rescue, but to lead ourselves along the particular means and trails of our existential predicaments, and to rescue ourselves by means of simple, everyday logics, or common sense.

Chapter X
THE 'RESCUER' AS THE UNCONSCIOUS SOLUTION TO LONELINESS

The 'Rescuer' in Samuel Beckett's "Waiting for Godot"

God represents the most popular rescuer ever used by humanity, despite the painful fact that nobody has ever seen or talked to God. In reality, when we think we are 'talking to God' – like when praying for instance – we are only talking to ourselves, as we *wait* for God's intervention and the consolidation of the so 'expected miracle'. This is an important aspect that Beckett has immortalised in his well-known play "Waiting for Godot"; after all, the name of 'God–ot',[57] chosen by the author, clearly points in that direction. I do not think it was by chance that Beckett wrote this play, but, in order to find some evidence that could provide a meaning, we must look into his emotional life, possibly during the first years of his existence, as well as his analysis with Bion, to gather some

---

[57] However, in a letter to actor Richardson, London's official censor, who barraged Beckett with questions about the play's characters, he explained that all he knew about the characters he had already said in the text of the play: 'I also told Richardson that if by Godot I had meant God I would [have] said God, and not Godot.' [Knowlson, Ibid, p. 172]. It is distinctly possible that Beckett could have used this argument in order to ease the difficulties he was already having with the censor, as he tried to produce the French play, *En attendant Godot*, in London, and did not wish to get snared into a religious controversy.

THE 'RESCUER' AS THE UNCONSCIOUS SOLUTION TO LONELINESS

clues about his own 'pre-conceptual trauma' and how such events could have influenced him to produce that play. Many times this play has been viewed through the lens of existentialism, religion, or 'philosophy of the absurd'; I favour this more fathomable investigation to provide an explanation of his play.[58]

It has been often indicated by reviewers, that *Waiting for Godot* is a drama where 'nothing happens' and yet it maintains a continuous sense of suspense that keeps people nailed to their chairs. Cohn (1967) had established that this play is

> ...a lucid testimony of nothingness. But while we are left cold by many dramas of intrigue in which a great deal happens, this 'nothing happens...' keeps us in suspense. [p. 106]

But why? What is contained in this play that carries the paradox of 'nothing happening' and, at the same time, fills us with attentiveness and concern? I will say that intuitively we might identify with the 'waiting' of two ordinary people – Vladimir and Estragon – who boundlessly anticipate someone who never appears, never anthropomorphises, in spite of their needs and deep sense of helplessness. Religion represents a commanding primeval establishment that through the years has used different means to proselytise; from coercion to threat, guilt, and even death. It is the

---

[58] Sartre, (cited by Cohn, 1967) considered that the play could have also referred to 'boredom'. He states: 'The psychological and social levels are transcended here; *Waiting for Godot* is a valuable contribution towards a metaphysics of boredom.' (p. 105) I believe, on the other hand, that 'boredom' is an 'emotional state' experienced by adults, as a direct consequence of 'unremembered memories' from childhood, associated with the relationship small children have with their mothers. The presence of the mother and interaction with her is the main subject of interest and distraction for all children. When the mother is absent, the child feels completely lost. It is this 'unremembered memory' of the 'absent mother' that later will determine the feeling of the adult's boredom.

endless 'waiting for a rescuer' that is continuously present within the depth of our unconscious, although we might not pay total attention to this longing, to the desire that someone or something will eventually save us from feeling helpless and lonely, similar to how our parents could have rescued us when we were children. I believe that it is the existence of this unconscious longing, present in all humans, that prompts the intuitive desire to identify with this infructuous 'waiting for Godot', and what keeps the audience completely enthralled in the play. Octavio Paz heartbreakingly described 'a lonely cry', which I have already quoted in the preface and will now repeat:

> ...Endless instant: to hear oneself cry in the middle of universal deafness...the feeling has never been erased, and never will be. It is not a wound, it is a hole. When I think of myself, I touch it: as I sense it, I feel it. Alien always and always present, never leaves me, presence without body, mute, invisible, perpetual witness of my life. He does not speak to me, but sometimes I hear what his silence says to me: ...you discovered your absence, your hole: you discovered yourself. You already know: you are dearth and search.

Beckett's 'Waiting for God'

Amid the endless ongoing historical clashes between Protestants and Catholics in Ireland – as well as in France and Spain – profound antimony had developed between the two groups. It is in this environment that Beckett's parents, May Roe and Bill Beckett, met. There is a story about their encounter:

> ...he [Bill Beckett] had fallen head over heels in love with a young woman named Eva Murphy, the daughter of a fairly

THE 'RESCUER' AS THE UNCONSCIOUS SOLUTION TO LONELINESS

> wealthy Catholic, William Martin Murphy...The Murphys were fiercely opposed to either of their children marrying into such deeply Protestant families: The Murphy man said he would despise...his daughter [who] could go on to the streets, he would never talk to her again, if she married Bill Beckett [who was Protestant]. [Knowlson, 1996, pp. 32–33]

As a consequence, Bill became deeply depressed, to the point that he was committed to Adelaide Hospital. It was in there that he met May Roe, who was working there as either a nurse or a nursing aide.

> May was at her best in periods of crisis, and her practical skills, no-nonsense approach, and genuine kindness and thoughtfulness seem to have quickly won over someone who was vulnerable to the attentions of this capable woman who offered him support as well as affection – and who came from a respectable Protestant family. She responded to his friendly banter, and in a matter of weeks they were engaged, and within the year, married. [Ibid, p. 33]

Samuel Beckett witnessed and attended three important deaths in his family: his father in 1933 when he was twenty-seven years old – this affected him deeply, as we shall see further on; the death of his mother in 1950 when he was forty-four and that of his brother Frank in 1954 when he was forty-eight were also very significant for him. The three of them did not die sudden deaths; they experienced life-compromising ailments that allowed a certain time of gradual increment of worsening before they passed away, allowing Beckett to witness their deterioration, perhaps wishing and 'waiting' for a miracle from God's intervention to take place. Bill Beckett was, according to Samuel, growing old 'with a very graceful philosophy', moving around as if he was still young: 'playing golf, swimming and walking up mountains'. (Knowlson, Ibid, p. 165). However, in mid-June 1933, he had a massive heart attack:

> The first attack did not kill him. But it put him to bed...made him feel very weak, miserable and helpless. Beckett washed him and shaved him...[Ibid]

Two weeks later, the doctor found him much better, and, in order to celebrate the good news,

> ...and probably to cheer up his father, Beckett put on the brightest clothes he could find...But hardly had the doctor left the house than Bill Beckett collapsed with another massive heart attack...he died about four o'clock in the afternoon. [Ibid] .

About May Beckett, his mother, who died on the evening of August 25, 1950, Bair (1978) wrote:

> All day long Beckett had sat beside her bed, watching her labored breathing, until he could stand it no more. Then he went for a walk...and when he returned to the nursing home, sat outside for a while on a bench, shivering in the evening wind. When he looked up at her window, he saw the shade go down, the signal that she had died. [p. 405]

Years later in his book "Krapp's Last Tape", Beckett refers to this experience about 'waiting' for her death:

> ...There I sat, in the biting wind, wishing she were gone...the blind went down...I happened to look up and there it was. All over and done with at last. [Cited by Bair, p. 406]

THE 'RESCUER' AS THE UNCONSCIOUS SOLUTION TO LONELINESS

Bair (Ibid) made further comments about Beckett's experience during this difficult time:

> His days passed in an exhausting, crushing depression brought on by long hours at her bedside. His nights were spent walking and talking with Geoffrey Thompson, to whom he complained bitterly of *the so-called God who would permit such suffering.*[59] [p. 405].

In several letters to Pamela Mitchell about the death of his brother Frank in 1954 – who died from terminal lung cancer – he decanted his unhappiness:

> ...week by week, charted his brother's sad, slow deterioration. These letters reflect his shifting awareness of time throughout this dreadful experience. At first, the days passed by very quickly, perhaps because there was so much to be done; then they began to slow down to a painful crawl, as change seemed imperceptible and what change there was could only be for the worse... '*Waiting [is] not so bad if you can fidget about. This is like waiting tied to a chair.*'[60] [Knowlson, 1996; p. 363]

The expression 'Nothing to be done', voiced by Estragon at the very beginning of the play, and often repeated by him and Vladimir during the rest of the performance, can be related to that lonely and painful waiting Beckett must have experienced during those long hours of uncertainty, perceiving the progressive deterioration of the closest and most loving persons in his life.

---

59 My italics.
60 My italics.

The Play

"Waiting for Godot" contains two acts with five characters: two scruffy friends, Vladimir and Estragon; Pozzo and Lucky, acting as a master and his slave; and a boy playing Godot's messenger. Vladimir and Estragon sustain a continuous and mundane dialogue, possibly representing how ordinary people communicate and struggle, attempting to cope in one way or the other with the everyday demands made by life and reality; possibly symbolising the 'universal man', as stated by Cormier and Pallister (1979, p. 5), although it could also be taken for an ongoing dialogue between two internal elements in Beckett's mind:[61] a 'needy, emotional and fundamental aspect' depicted by Estragon, and a more 'intellectual and independent one' represented by Vladimir. The boy, acting as Godot's messenger, could be equated to an angel or God's emissary, as well as a cleric or something of that sort. It is possible that this could have represented the way some people select to connect with God as a 'rescuer', like believing when they are praying that they are directly communicating with God!

Beckett's relationship with his father was not without complications, however. Indeed, the characters in "Waiting for Godot" help illuminate their relationship with the ongoing dialogue between Estragon and Vladimir representing two internal elements in Beckett's mind:[62] a 'needy, emotional and fundamental aspect', depicted by Estragon, and a more 'intellectual and independent one', represented by Vladimir. Referring to Bill's attitude towards his wife and children, Bair (1978) remarked that he

> ...was not without a streak of *stubborn cruelty that often took the form of a relentless insistence on physical perfection in his*

---

[61] See Cohn, R., 1967, in References.
[62] See Cohn, R., 1967, in References.

THE 'RESCUER' AS THE UNCONSCIOUS SOLUTION TO LONELINESS

> *sons and compliance with outward forms of genteel behavior...*[63] [Ibid, p. 13].

And further on:

> ...for he had [Bill] a streak of genuine cruelty hidden behind a façade of masculine bravado. It showed when he forced the two little boys to match his prodigious athletic feats in ways which strained their bodies beyond a reasonable limit of endurance. [Ibid. p. 16]

Knowlson (Ibid) also refers to the terror Beckett experienced in the presence of Balfe, the road repairman in Foxrock, the town where the Becketts resided:

> Whose terrifying stare was enough to make Beckett quake as a small boy and scuttle indoors. 'I remember the rock man...A man called Balfe. He used to look at me. He terrified me. I can still remember how he frightened me.' [p. 41]

Beckett mentioned Balfe in some of his writings, like in "From an Abandoned Work", where he stated: 'The day I saw the look I got from Balfe, I went in terror of him as a child.' And sometime later in "From to End Yet Again", he said: 'he will confuse his mother with whores, his father with a roadman named Balfe.' Obviously, if Bill Beckett was confused with the terrorising roadman Balfe, it meant that the relationship between Beckett and his father was not so harmonious and relaxing after all. In the play, Pozzo is confused with Godot when he arrived at the scene:

---

63 My italics.

Estragon: Is that him?
Vladimir: Who?
Estragon: Er... (*trying to remember the name*)
Vladimir: Godot?
Estragon: Yes
Pozzo: I present myself: Pozzo....
Pozzo: Who is Godot?
Estragon: Godot?
Pozzo: You took me for Godot...

Pozzo's cruelty is underscored in the treatment of Lucky, using epithets like 'pig' and hog', which could have reproduced the sort of reproachful statement sometimes aggressive parents concerned with etiquette will use to correct children's 'terrible' table manners. In addition to Pozzo's arrogance and disparagement towards Lucky, the use of the whip is also very relevant.

Curiously, Beckett often described what he considered a 'perfect childhood' and at a given moment during an interview he stated: 'You might say I had a happy childhood...My parents did everything that they could to make a child happy...My father did not beat me, nor did my mother run away from home.' However, Bair (Ibid) with clear intuition added: 'Perhaps the interior realities of the situation did indeed belie the exterior trappings of the perfect childhood.' (p. 14) 'However, his mother did beat him severely and constantly, while his father was never there.' (Ibid, p. 16). And we could add that Bill Beckett besides being absent was also capable of inducing nameless terror. Bill was described as very inconsistent; he could be extremely friendly but also very violent. He was described by Bair (1978) as a 'round-faced, ruddy-complected man with a booming voice and a penchant for backslapping that literally knocked the wind from any of his brawny buddies'. (pp. 5–6)

THE 'RESCUER' AS THE UNCONSCIOUS SOLUTION TO LONELINESS

> He had a highly developed sense of humor, a ready wit, and a bonhomie...This was accompanied by a fiery temper that could flare up quickly from time to time. He was known to have found a cat in his bed and thrown it out of the window. [Knowlson, Ibid, p. 31]

The children hardly saw him as he was most of the time busy at his work, or entertaining friends at his club in the evenings, a situation that was remarked by Bair (Ibid), who stated that, 'often they did not see him from weekend to weekend, except briefly at breakfast'. (p. 10). It has been often said that one important psychological conflict in Beckett was the possessive and domineering attitude his mother exercised over him (Anzieu, 1986; Bleándonu, 1994; Stevens, 2005) although, as far as I know, it has never been said that Beckett's dependency on his mother was possibly a consequence of his father's absence. As I have often expressed in this book, women – who provide life and unconditional love – carry the baby for nine months just like another of their internal organs, and are biologically inclined to become possessive and to exercise dependency. The fathers, on the other hand, remaining as an 'outsider' during those early years of their children's life, are capable of breaking the mother's natural symbiosis and providing hope and independence to the child.

By extension, in Freud (1927)'s view, God represents the adult unconscious manifestation of the inner child's longing for being rescued by the idealised father. It should not be any surprise then that, to use a psychological comprehension of "Waiting for Godot", Beckett continuously introduced in his plays and novels personal memories from his own childhood, thereby describing different aspects of his family and of himself.

Beckett and Bion

After his father's death, Samuel Beckett consulted Wilfred Bion in 1934 due to a series of symptoms that could be considered as hysterical: 'severe anxiety, claustrophobia, fear of madness, heart palpitations, night sweats, insomnia, depression and on occasions, even total paralysis'. (Knowlson, 1996, p. 369; Miller, 2013, p. 4) These symptoms appeared shortly after his father's death from a massive heart attack in June 1933. This is what Beckett has to say about this difficult time:

> After my father's death, I had trouble psychologically. The bad years were between when I had to crawl home in 1932 and after my father's death in 1933. I will tell you how it was. I was walking down Dawson Street. And I felt I couldn't go on. It was a strange experience I can't really describe. I found I couldn't go on moving. So I went into the nearest pub and got a drink just to stay still. And I felt I needed help. So I went to Geoffrey Thompson's surgery. Geoffrey wasn't there; he was at Lower Baggot Street hospital; so I waited for him. When he got there, I was standing by the door. He gave me a look over and found nothing physically wrong. Then he recommended psychoanalysis for me. Psychoanalysis was not allowed in Dublin at that time. It was not legal. So, in order to have psychoanalysis, you had to come to London. [Knowlson, 1996, p. 167]

Beckett was twenty-seven years old when his father died. However, he was acutely affected by his loss to the point that he might have identified himself with his dead father when he abruptly became paralysed. Afterwards, he produced symptoms likeminded with terror of death, possibly related to guilt as if he felt unconsciously accountable, similar to how children – analogous to Beckett – develop phobias, when, out of anger towards their parents, they magically think they have killed them just by thinking or wishing it. These emotions can also be often observed during processes of bereavement, when there are ambivalent feelings towards the deceased, mostly aggression, which induce guilt and unconscious need for punishment. I have previously referred to a patient who developed arthritis after her husband passed away, as if she unconsciously was trying to 'paralyse herself' out of guilt for being alive. (López-Corvo, 2014, p.141), (Anzieu, p. 164)

Samuel Beckett also disparaged his father for being 'absolutely non-intellectual', for abandoning school at the age of fifteen and being put to work as a surveyor in the construction business of his family. According to Knowlson (Ibid), in an interview in July 1992, Samuel said about his father: 'He had a big case of books, Dickens and Encyclopedias that he never opened. He used to read Edgar Wallace.' (p. 31). Knowlson has also stated that in: "Dream of Fair to Middling Women", one of his early novels, Beckett referred to his father in the following manner:

> ...it was with a mixture of amusement and envy that he described his father's way of reading: 'His father assembled his arsenal of cold pipes,[64] turned on the book, connected up, and it did the rest. That was the way to read – find out the literary voltage that suits you and switch on the current of the book...He sat motionless in the armchair under the singing lamp, absorbed and null. The pipes went out, one after another...he heard nothing that was said in the room...If you asked him next day what the book was like he could not tell you." [Knowlson, Ibid, p. 31]

---

64 The use of pipes is also present in Pozzo.

Undesired Consequences from the Need of a 'Rescuer'

In some of my presentations about Bion's concept on links, I have used the Swedish film "As it is in Heaven", only three minutes from the start and analogous time from the end of the movie. At the opening, there is a little boy of around ten years of age, who is a violin virtuoso and who provokes a great amount of envy from his classmates. In one scene they find him playing his violin hidden in a wheat field, they beat him badly and even masturbate over him. Distressed by this, the family moves to a different town. As an adolescent, he suffers the loss of his mother when she is struck and killed by a car while crossing the street. With time, he becomes an internationally well-known musician, composer, and director, but also develops a heart condition that at a particular moment forces him to retire. He returns to his hometown and buys the school where he was originally tormented, eventually becoming director of the local choir. Towards the end of the movie, there is an international choral competition, but he is very late and the singers from his choir are becoming very impatient. At the same time, he is strongly bicycling and finally arrives, but while climbing the stairs he collapses and falls on the floor and, while he seems to be dying, he had a fantasy of being in the wheat field where he finds himself as a little boy. He pictures himself as the little boy he used to be and holds him tied, as if he was finally capable of 'rescuing' the helpless little boy in him that he used to be. *At this particular moment, in all the presentations I have made, most of the people in the audience, shed some tears.* What precisely makes this fragment of the film so poignant? I don't believe the tears are a product of our existential aloneness, from what Heidegger has already labelled the 'Dasein'; it is more related to the sense of loneliness we all experienced as children, when we felt betrayed by our angry (disrespectable, abusive, impatient, and so on) parents, and there

THE 'RESCUER' AS THE UNCONSCIOUS SOLUTION TO LONELINESS

was nobody else to turn to. It is this loneliness that remains within the core of our pre-conceptual trauma, which will induce in everybody the unconscious need to search for an outside 'rescuer', like God for instance, or Godot, as Beckett preferred, without being able to reflect that perhaps the only one capable of rescuing ourselves is only *ourselves!* Just as the movie had depicted it. In the film, the power of this image portrays the ontological fact that we are completely alone and that there is nobody else to turn to, and it is the power of this realisation that crystallises tears in our eyes. It is in the end a by-product of the confusion between the personal *loneliness* resulting from the accident of our pre-conceptual trauma, and the ontological fatalism of our existential *alones* in which all humans are immersed.

Counting on outside 'rescuers', instead of relying on ourselves, can often present serious consequences. Turning to God or religion may awake unconscious infantile emotions of sibling rivalry, which often promotes wars and terrorism in an attempt to prove which one of their 'invented "rescuer" gods' is better than the others, as has been the case in Ireland or the Middle East. Indiscriminate use of medical doctors and medicines might have serious health consequences, as may the sexual abuse of children in the hands of paedophile priests, or the existence of 'unresolved mourning' and its emotional consequences in those who use 'dead relatives' as a form of 'rescuer', as well as the hazard of crime, delinquency and drug trafficking in individuals who privilege money and accumulation of wealth to rescue themselves. Likewise, the use of idealisation as a form of defence, as an unconscious remnant from childhood at the time when our parents were our superheroes, could often result in self-debasing, guilt, masochism and chronic anxiety. Small children, when considered as 'wise babies', often become a form of rescuer, something that could induce parents to give to their children names of well-known historical characters, like Napoleon, Alexander, Julius Cesar or the name of saints, and so on. However, when that child fails to provide that hope, parental aggression is sometimes the result. Consider, for instance, cases of 'psychogenic autism'. This matter will require some explanation and, although it is probable that some readers could disagree with me, I invite them to think about why are there more autistic boys than girls, or why children are able to improve their autistic features after an 'affectionate nanny' takes over their ministration. I believe that 'psychogenic autism' represents the child's identification or response – usually by boys – to a mother's projective identification who, as a form of 'passive aggression', has withdrawn her affection using obsessive defences in order to ward off filicidal impulses, induced by her disappointment and narcissistic injury at having given birth to an organic child.[65] I base this statement on clinical observations, as well as family studies and empirical findings such as the comparison between 'autistic psychosis' (Kanner, 1943) on one hand, and 'symbiotic psychosis' (Mahler, 1972) on the other. I have observed the incidence of 'autistic psychosis' is more prevalent in northern countries such as Canada, while 'symbiotic psychosis' is more common to tropical countries like Venezuela. My hypothesis is that 'autistic psychosis' arises from the ego's different forms of defence, which are employed in order to avoid the narcissistic pain that mothers experience when not being able to resolve their unconscious feelings of phallic envy and the need of a 'rescuer' after giving birth to an organic child. In other words, these usually very ambitious mothers feel very ashamed and disappointed when they give birth to a child who is mentally and/or physically limited, since they shelter high expectation for their child's performance due to their

---

65 Some of these concepts were previously presented in the paper "The Minotaur and his Labyrinth", read at the Montreal Children Hospital annual meeting, in 1989.

THE 'RESCUER' AS THE UNCONSCIOUS SOLUTION TO LONELINESS

own need to fulfil their 'narcissistic absence' from not 'having a penis'; moreover, an extraordinary penis that will make them exult with pride, and 'rescue' them from a delusional state of total ignominious feeling of non-existence. They shelter the strong will to give birth to an 'extraordinary child', usually a boy. This may explain why boys, on average, are five to fifteen times more likely to have autism than girls are.

Kanner's original description, and most of all his definition of the 'refrigerator mother' as one who lacks maternal warmth, was used to illustrate the cause of obsessive autistic detachment. This hypothesis prompted many researchers to sway to the other extreme, playing devil's advocate when they expressed that much responsibility was weighed on the parents who were already suffering the birth of a sick and difficult child. In any case, the fact that 'psychogenic autism' improves with psychoanalytical psychotherapy makes me think that the environment is determinant and that Kanner's original statement is still germane. The mechanics of the maternal rejection and the child's identification with it are difficult to observe; they are so personal, so intimate, and so specific to the mother-child relationship that I have previously referred to it as the 'schizoid secret'. (López-Corvo, 1995)

There is also a form of rescuer based on the interaction between the traumatised and the non-traumatised states, where the former plays the role of a 'rescuer' to the latter, which remains passive and helpless. Peter, a case I have already mentioned in Chapter V, is a patient who often produced degrading sexual fantasies directed at me whenever I elaborated on an interpretation. The 'traumatised state' was represented by an angry and revengeful child that had convinced the thinking, logical adult, or non-traumatised state in him, that this child was the true *rescuer* he never had, capable of saving the inner helpless child in him, and that such revengeful assaults were the only hope he could harbour in order to destroy his inner parents projected in the transference. To avoid repetitions, I would like to refer the reader to the case of Peter in Chapter V, which could provide more clarity to these statements.

Longing for the absent breast becomes a tyrannical presence of an absence, a form of defence against the terrible pain of containing the original absence. I believe this to be a universal type of resistance, where a sort of vicious circle trap or catch-22 is produced: the incapacity to contain the pain of the loss induces a powerful need for an outside rescuer. The rescue is always doomed to fail because it is impossible to fulfil a non-existent traumatic experience from the past. This failure generates the search for a new rescuer who also fails, and on it goes.

Chapter XI
LONELINESS AND THE OEDIPUS COMPLEX OR PARENTS AS 'RESCUERS'

> *Every new arrival on this planet is faced with the task of mastering the Oedipus complex.*
> — Sigmund Freud
> (1905, SE, VII, p.226, n. 1.)

The Four Pillars of the Oedipus Complex

With amazing accuracy Freud established that the Oedipus complex is always in the centre of any form of mental conflict.[66] There are at least *four main pillars* that sustain this complex:

i) The *five characters*, fatalistically predetermined and always present: *the father, the mother, the child, the crossroad where the murder is committed, and the bed where incest takes place*.

ii) The *narrative*, always particular and determined by process of identification, either cultural or biological: cultural because it

---

66 According to Bion (1974) any myth, like Oedipus, can be represented by the formula: 'K(ξ)', where K stands for a constant that is conscious and saturated – like the presence of always the same characters in the myth – and ξ which characterises what is variable, private, unsaturated and unconscious, i.e. the narrative, of how the characters have interacted in the myth. (p. 23)

is modelled following the specific characteristic of the individual's pre-conceptual trauma;[67] biological because of the mechanism of 'object choice'. In a 'positive Oedipus object choice' the boy child will select the mother, and the girl will prefer the father. A 'negative Oedipus object choice' centres on the opposite, where individuals prefer those of the same gender as observed in homosexuality. The main natural difference between heterosexuality and homosexuality centers on procreation. This process is guaranteed by the mother's 'narcissistic dearth' over lacking a penis that always induces 'phallic envy'. *This mechanism of the mother's phallic envy represents the core of the Oedipus Complex*, because, in the process of parental identification towards their children, the mother will prefer the boy to complete her narcissistic absence (or phallic envy), a choice that will induce the boys to favour her, and later, when they become adults, to desire women; a need and preference that will also cause the father to choose his daughters, in a similar way as he originally was desired by his mother as a child, and, as a consequence, for the daughter to favour him, and in adulthood to prefer men. In general there is more preference shown for the mother than the father, because mothers are the first object choice in the life of every human being.

iii) The third pillar consists of what the Greeks referred to as *Ananke*, destiny or necessity, representing Freud's 'repetition compulsion', meaning the inexorable and unconscious recurrent 'necessity' of the Oedipus complex to be always present. In Sophocles' account, the oracle told Oedipus that

---

[67] Paradoxically, pre-conceptual traumas also become at the same time a decisive factor that organises the mind, a '*selected fact*' in Bion's terminology, which outlines significant aspects of the characteristics and identity of all human beings. (See: López-Corvo, 2014, p. 23)

he would be the cause of his parents' death' and, believing that his 'adopted' parents King Polybus and Queen Merope from Corinth were his true parents, he decided to move to Thebe in order to spare their lives, not knowing that in fact by doing so he was going to fulfil his fate.

iv) The fourth pillar refers to the 'mechanisms of defence' used by the ego to guard itself from three main closely interrelated oedipal anxieties: *exclusion, castration and persecutory or guilt-ridden anxiety*. Different from the 'characters', the 'narrative' and the 'fate' – which are mostly unconscious – the 'mechanisms of defence' are in great part conscious and obvious, prompting specialists to use them in order to classify psychopathology; however, they are only unspecific symptoms that point to a hidden (unconscious) meaning, whose specific nature they never reveal. It will be similar to how the fever could disclose an infection but is unable to determine the precise aetiology of the germs in question. In summary, defences are generally descriptive, not meta-psychological, and very much *geographically determined*.

Process of Identification

Identification is an extension of imitation, because imitation results when the child replicates gestures produced by the adult, while identification appears once imitation is repeated without the presence of the external stimulus, representing a form of mental evolution that has moved from the 'sensory-motor to the representative'. Such dialectical interaction between ego and superego is also the regular architecture of the reciprocal link between transference and countertransference that are always reproduced via projective and introjective identifications.

I would like to insist on this aspect of identification, because I feel that it has not been emphasised enough. The structuring of the Oedipus complex involves a dialectical process of mutual identifications between children and their parents, which progressively become introjected as internal representation, *where the ego depicts the child, and the superego symbolises the parents.* As internal part-objects, they will for ever and continuously repeat the same dialectical interaction that once took place between the child and the parents. Such interaction, which continuously repeats intra-psychically between ego and superego or in relation to external objects using mechanisms of projective identification, represents the basis where the pre-conceptual traumas are eventually established. Laplanche and Pontalis (1967) had referred, although very succinctly, to the mutual identification present between parents and children when they said:

> ...we are led to assign an essential role in the constitution of a given Oedipus complex to the other poles of this relationship – the unconscious desires of both parents, seduction, and the relations between the parents...at least as much as any particular parental image – are destined to be internalised and to survive in the structure of the personality. [p. 186]

Unresolved parental oedipal issues induced by their particular pre-conceptual traumas will determine the manner in how they interact with their children, and, at the same time, of how children will identify with them, a situation that will also structure the particular 'narrative' of the child's pre-conceptual trauma. As specified above, mothers are moved by either castration anxiety, phallic envy or the need for a 'rescuer', as conditions that will encourage them to unconsciously prefer the boys over the girls; while fathers, unconsciously motivated by that partiality already exercised towards them by their mothers, will favour their own daughters in return; a condition that often induces competition with their sons.

LONELINESS AND THE OEDIPUS COMPLEX OR PARENTS AS 'RESCUERS'

At the same time, driven by their helplessness, loneliness, and impotence, children are incessantly on the watch for any parental form of behaviour, with the sole purpose of exercising complete control, as a defence to compensate their feelings of impotence, helplessness and loneliness.

Some clinical examples might be helpful. Alicia, a woman three years older than her younger brother, was eight years old when her parents got divorced. Her father, who was rather more selective and overprotective of her than her brother, moved to a different city shortly after the divorce, a condition that marked Alicia for life, since she then interpreted his departure as a rejection of her. She unconsciously felt that she has been the 'perpetrator of something terrible against him'. It was a condition that induced in her appalling and unconscious feelings of total desolation and guilt, deepened by her mother's unfair predilection towards her younger brother, something that was further increased after the divorce. This state of affairs was possibly the core of her pre-conceptual trauma. At the age of thirty-five she married D, a man whose character she described as shy, very reserved and rather schizoid. According to her, he was very different from her father whom she considered 'aggressive' and a 'kind of womanizer'. At one point I said to her that perhaps her choice of a man who was so different from her father, was an expression of her need to have a man she could control, because of her fear that he could abandoned her as her father once did. A year into her marriage she had a son and five years later she delivered a girl. She created a special bond with Antoine, her son, as if she had projected into him the part of her she felt was abandoned by her father. She provided him with the 'exaggerated' attention she unconsciously wished she could have had from her absent father. After her daughter was born, Antoine resented her presence and started to make more demands on her, like wanting his mother to sleep with him in his bed, or for him to squeeze into his parents bed in the middle of the night; he also insisted on seeing his mother naked and showing her his penis. I felt that the mother's pre-conceptual trauma, related to how her father had interacted with her and how he then completely and abruptly disappeared, marked her for life and also determined the way she interacted with her older son, structuring his own Oedipus complex and pre-conceptual trauma, as well as his future behaviour.

'Perversion' or the Obscure Corner of the Oedipus Complex

All children have the biological need to possess and control their mother, and mostly boys, who are, as I have already stated, usually chosen by the mother to complete her narcissistic absence of a phallus. When the child experiences the 'absence' of the mother, either in relation to the father or due to the birth of another child, the excluded child will attempt to find any other way in order to gain the mother back again, even more if these 'ways' are *forbidden paths*, behind the father and the siblings' back. The creation of a secret between the mother and child makes the child feel more special. Children are naturally 'polymorphous perverse', as Freud has originally described them; meaning that they are always open to any experience, as long as it does not hurt! But before we go any further into this subject we should clarify some semantic aspects. 'Perversion' was originally used by Freud in relation to sexuality, to describe how procreation, the main purpose of sexuality, could become subordinated to foreplay; or, in other words, how the main end of sexuality is 'perverted'. However, this original and innocent description introduced by Freud has become somewhat of a 'bad word' and a serious offence. I believe that what has compelled this word to become unfriendly is not the meaning

Freud had associated with it, but the unconscious guilt that always accompanies the transgression involved in the act.

I believe perversion represents the 'dark side of the Oedipus complex', a particular space that has been fashioned following essentials from the 'pre-conceptual trauma'. The purpose of perversion is to establish, at any cost, a secret *complicity* outside the limit of what is lawful, in order for the helpless child to control and dominate the object of their desire. It is a defence children always use – mostly boys – in order to deal with feelings of exclusion and impotence, usually supported by the mother's complicity because of her need to use her child – following Freud's equation of 'boy = faeces = phallus' – to complement her 'narcissistic absence'. Although perversion has been associated only with sexual drive, the truth is that children's provocation to their mothers with the intention of controlling her is not only sexual but also aggressive, possibly because the main instrument used to achieve such a response would be anything that generates a reaction from the mother. The difference between the prevalence of sexual pleasure over aggressive kind of domination will depend on how parents identify with their children, something always contingent to the structure of the parents own 'pre-conceptual trauma'. It is habitually the consequence of the mother's inconsistency, when for a given reason she overindulges in her relationship towards a child and then withdraws, usually after the birth of another child. This condition is often observed in males who were the older and were preceded by a particular situation where the mother might overprotect them, like the death of a previous child, or when the mother's pre-conceptual trauma is tinged by early separation or abandonment, and she projects an internal 'abandoned element' in her onto that child, or when there is a significant age difference between the older child and the one that follows. Children might then react either using sensual manipulation to gain their mother back, or, if that fails, they could use threatening acting out. The total or partial absence of the father plays a significant role in this mechanism.[68]

The fact that both drives – sex and aggression – are compromised in perversion could result in sadomasochistic behaviour which is always present in any form of this pathology, where aggression is often hidden in the form of unconscious guilt, anxiety and need for punishment. In the case of Alicia, whom I have just mentioned, her son Antoine attempted to control her first by seduction, and when he felt that that had failed, he resorted to act out with the purpose of frightening her. Shortly after the birth of his sister, Antoine had a dream he considered as 'very scary': *someone unknown was on the other side of the street offering candies. He went to cross the road to get the candy and kept tripping and falling; a car was coming and he was going to be hit by it.* Resenting the separation and birth of a new child, Antoine was attempting to gain back his mother's attention by making her feel very concerned, because he knew how worried she would be if she knew that he was accepting candy from a stranger, crossing the street without assistance and being nearly hit by a car! The dream was an attempt to gain back the sense of essentiality he felt was now lost with the birth of his younger sister. I believe that what he qualified as 'very scary' was not the dream itself, but the terror about his anger for no longer being his mother's 'narcissistic completion'.

'School phobias', often present in latency, usually resolve at eleven or twelve years of age, when the mind of the child reaches the stage of 'formal operations' and is capable then of using logical means to solve emotional confusions. This phobia is usually a consequence of conflictive patterns present in parents as a

---

[68] The role of the father has been discussed in more detail in Chapter VIII.

product of their own pre-conceptual traumas. A nine year old little girl developed crisis of anxiety at the time of going to school, or in situations when she was separated from her mother. There was an older boy who did not present any symptomatology similar to his sister. The mother revealed that she had argued with her husband because he often showed more preference for the girl than for the boy, which resulted in frequent friction between the two: 'He will talk to her and explain issues from his work, as if she was an adult capable of understanding what he said,' expressed the mother. I said that perhaps the father was unconsciously providing the girl with a sense of importance that could have induced a feeling of competition with her mother. She might wish for her to 'disappear', to 'go away', in order for her to take her place. However, since she used magic means to deal with her natural feelings of helplessness, she might have felt that she could in reality make her mother disappear, and the only means she had to know that her mother was still there was to 'see' her, because when she did not see her, she became terrified thinking that she could have killed her with her thoughts. The girl felt very ambivalent about these desires, because at the same time she loved her mother and felt very guilty for 'hurting her'.

Chapter XII
WHY SELF-ENVY?

> *I said that he felt so envious of himself and of me for being able to work together to make him feel better that he took the pair of us into him as a dead piece of iron and a dead floor that came together not to give him life but to murder him.*
>
> — Bion (1959)
> (In *Second Thoughts*, 1967, p. 97)

Introduction

Envy is an emotional state present in all individuals; it is the direct consequence of the uneven interaction between the *helplessness* of the child and the *supremacy* of the parents who are always idealised by their children. If we were born as adults, nobody would ever experience envy. 'Self-envy' is perhaps not the best appellation we could use to designate this mechanism, because I am not referring to envy towards the self, but to envy that is experienced 'between internal parts' or, to be more precise, the envy the 'traumatised state' experiences towards the 'non-traumatised', or, in Bion's terms, the 'alpha function'. I have already referred in Chapter IV to how the process of identification is always the product of a dialectical interaction between the ego, representing the child, and the superego, signifying the parents. Whatever takes place between the child and their parents, and vice versa, remains permanently registered in the mind once it is introjected and identified with. This determines the dynamics of the pre-conceptual trauma, which will then, as an eternal present, repeat compulsively forever as the 'traumatised state'.

WHY SELF-ENVY?

    Any form of abuse, either aggressive or sexual, will induce in the child an intense sense of loneliness and helplessness, and, as a consequence, the need to split the parents into good and bad, or, to be more specific, *rescuers* and *accusers*, respectively. However, when such fragmentation fails, it create a circularity between projections and introjections following mechanisms already described by Klein. If children experience a feeling of 'helplessness' they will then harvest the need of a 'rescuer', using idealisation as a form of defence; however, this idealisation could promote envy and the need to attack the idealised object. The guilt induced by this action will again provoke the need to incorporate the idealised revengeful object, and to project the helpless part in an ongoing circularity. With time, everybody will become an adult, although internally 'the child' or 'traumatised state' will remain as confused as it was sensed in the past as a child, when the emotions were repressed and only beta elements were available; meaning that the same interaction that once took place between the child and their parents will now take place internally, between the 'traumatised state' (child part) and the adult that the individual has now become, or 'non-traumatised state'.

    Internal envy, envy between the parts or self-envy will then present as a repetition of whatever the child had originally envied in their parents, especially if the latter had excessively and aggressively exercised their power over the fragility of the former. There are usually two forms of recurrent dreams in childhood, although it can be present in adults also. One is about finding coins on the ground; the other is about flying; both are related to feelings of helplessness and powerlessness. Coins because children associate money with adult's control for procuring anything, something they are unable to attain; flying because flight is related to power and freedom, something we observe in the mythology of the 'superheroes' like Superman.

Afterwards, when we reach adulthood we become similar to how our parents were at the time when we were children, like having their power to decide, or the capacity to reason – or alpha function – as well as control, achievement, freedom and so on. We could then, often unconsciously, direct the same envy we once experienced towards our adult parents, at the 'internalised parents' inside our mind, and enviously attack our own capacity to think logically, to control, to achieve, to be creative and free, just as we once enviously attacked our real parents in the past. A continuous envious attack on alpha-function is a total hindrance that will always delay or completely obstruct the capacity for recovery.

Although difficult to acknowledge, 'self-envy' is in reality a much more prevalent mechanism than we might think. In the first place, envy is always the consequence, or the projection, of a private longing, because we always envy what we idealise, what we wish for and feel we need. Envy is triggered not by what the other has, but by what the other has that we feel we need or want. In other words, *all forms of envy are originally 'self-envy'*: whether it is envy of wealth, beauty, power, youth, or position, it always stems from our childhood experience of seeing our parents in possession of something we feel we need or want but as a child we are not allowed to have. The real interaction between the one who envies and the one who is envied is always a form of projection or 'transference', a mirage that originates in our private hunger for our wants and needs that we have projected on the other.

Envy's Internal Route

Envy is the product of three main defences used by the ego: i) *splitting* of the object in 'good idealised' and 'bad persecutory'; ii) *projection* of the 'good *idealised* object'; iii) *introjection* of the 'bad persecutory'. Let us examine these defences in more detail: i) *splitting*: we are all born with our mind split in bits, and, to integrate it, to put our mind together, could take most of a person's life. Since this process in itself is just a possibility, it is usually never completely achieved; ii) *projection*: following Klein, there are initially two main part-objects: the object present or 'good object' and the presence of the absence of the object or 'bad object,' which, due to the incapacity of the child to integrate, remains separated as two different entities. While the good object is kept inside, the bad object will be always attacked and projected outside, from whence it will threaten the ego-inducing anxiety and paranoid feelings; the whole process represents what Klein has described as the 'paranoid-schizoid position'; iii) *idealisation*: however, since most of the ego's defences fail, the anxiety produced by the 'persecution' of the projected 'bad persecutory object' will induce the need to idealise the 'internalised good object' as a kind of 'protector' or magic 'rescuer', a defence that will also fail due to the supremacy of reality, because, after all, children are in fact helpless and depend on their 'powerful parents' for everything. The projection into the parents of the idealised object will then trigger *envious* attacks from the child towards their power, as well as retaliatory anxiety and guilt in the child, from the bad-persecutory part-object that has been projected in them. This will induce an emotional circularity or vicious circle: introjection of the bad object, projection of the idealised, envy and attack towards the 'idealised object' projected, guilt, introjection of the 'bad object' and masochistic need for punishment. As adults, this interaction between the ego and the parents will be introjected and continuously reproduced internally, between the ego and the superego. The envy then, instead of being focused on the 'external parents', is now directed to aspects of the superego that Freud once referred to as the 'ideal ego', representing the same idealised features that were previously idealised in the 'external parents'. The envious interaction between these internalised elements that once took place with the external parents and is now reproduced with the internalised parents is what I have referred to as 'envy between the parts' or 'self-envy'.

A forty year old woman, the youngest and only girl of three children, consulted because of an occasional crisis of bulimia, when she would secretly over-eat and then vomit. It was usually triggered by frustration, in situations when, according to her, she felt powerless. She stated that her mother was very critical and aggressive in comparison to her father, who she described as soft, usually absent and dominated by her mother. She felt that her mother openly privileged her older brothers while she was very critical and demanding of her. I said to her that she was very *envious* of her brothers and wished she was a boy. As a consequence, she tried to steal their penis by continuously swallowing it, as if she was confusing it with her mother's breast, and then, out of fear and guilt, she would vomit it up. It was as if, within the traumatised part, she confused the penis with the breast as well as the mind, and her mouth with her anus, because the ingestion and the vomiting were too immediate, too close to each other, different from the normal function of mouth and anus.

She was married and divorced and had other relationships that were usually terminated because she was critical and always found imperfections in her partners. Out of self-envy she exhibited a need to destroy the 'harmonious couple', as a repetition of what she wished to do as a child to her parents' 'loving couple', or to the relationship her mother had with her brothers, mostly the older one. As the therapy progressed, she acted out by being late or missing sessions without calling. She tried to find faults in the analysis and even tried to induce them; she would, for instance, refer to a dream in which she was having sexual relations and provided details about it, and then turn around on the couch to see my reaction; at another time, she overpaid to see if I would acknowledge the mistake, in order to test my honesty. I said to her that she feared I could be someone reliable who she could have trusted, but this would make her very envious, so she was trying to smear my behaviour by making me dishonest and unreliable, and by stealing my 'analytical ability' or my 'penis-knowledge' that could have liberated her, and then dismissed me as she did with her husband and boyfriends, and then tried to vomit her guilt. It reminded me of Meltzer's concept of the 'perversion of transference': 'if I interpreted her behaviour, I was against her, but if I said nothing, I was an accomplice'. However, her main problem was that, by doing this, she completely isolated herself, made herself helpless and lonely, as she felt she was as a little girl who enviously attacked her parents. The main subject was that the attack was on herself, on her well-being as a form of 'self-envy'. There was an ongoing divergence and competition against her husband and children, mostly her adolescent daughter. I had the feeling that she very much envied her husband's intellect – similar to how she envied her father's – and her daughter's beauty, youth, and indomitable struggle for independence. At a particular moment, she presented a dream: *she was escaping with her husband from Zombies who were going to suck their brains. They arrived at a building, some sort of factory, and went inside to hide but could not close the door. She saw lockers and decided to put her husband inside and locked the door with a padlock; but then she thought that if the Zombies came in, they might be able to get her, because it was impossible for her to lock herself in from inside, but also, if the Zombies killed her, then there was nobody to free her husband.*

I said to her that her dream seemed to depict a dangerous, 'locked' kind of situation, as if, for her, there was not a way out, like a sort of 'catch-22' dilemma. There was an envious and destructive part of her that was trying to destroy her 'thinking brain', or alpha function, represented by her 'intellectual' husband; but there was no way out, because she would not be able to lock herself, and her 'thinking capacity' (alpha function) would be destroyed (eaten), and if she locked her husband and the zombies ate her brain, he would never be able to liberate himself either. It was very much like her bulimia: she steals the idealised penis of her father, siblings, and husband, in order to obtain a thinking instrument (alpha function) that could have unbound her, but then she felt so guilty that she had to vomit it up again, and castrate herself in an endlessly psychotic process. In the dream, she destroys her 'alpha function' that she would need in order to liberate her 'alpha function'! It was a very conflictive form of 'self-envy' which I feel is at the core of the pre-conceptual trauma present in bulimia. To this form of imprisonment, Bion (1967) said the following:

> ... His sense impressions appear to have suffered mutilation of a kind which would be appropriate had they been attacked as the breast is felt to be attacked in the sadistic phantasies of the infant. The patient feels imprisoned in the state of mind he has achieved, and unable to escape from it because he feels he lacks the apparatus of awareness of reality [alpha function] which is both the key to escape and the freedom to which he would escape. The sense of imprisonment is intensified by the menacing presence of the expelled fragments within whose planetary movements he is contained. [p. 51]

Self-envy and Negative Links

I have considered the presence of an important form of communication between split parts based on the existence of false or 'negative links'. I believe self-envy is a sort of negative link, or minus hate (–H), similar to –K and –L, representing a type of communication between split parts, within the traumatised stated, following logic founded on the paranoid-schizoid position. Bion said little about minus hate (-H) and minus love (-L), in comparison to what he said about minus knowledge (-K). He associated negative links to the 'absence of something', although it is not clear what exactly that 'something' meant to Bion (1963). About minus K (-K), Bion said more, like the dynamic observed in what he described as 'reversible perspective', a condition where both patient and therapist run on parallel tracks without ever really communicating with each other, a sort of 'dialogue between the deaf'. Minus K also represents the central mechanism present in intellectualisation as a form of defence. 'The first problem,' said Bion (1967), 'is to see what can be done to increase scientific rigor by establishing the nature of minus K (- K), minus L (-L), and minus H (-H)'. [pp. 51-2].

I believe positive links, like +K, +L and +H, represent factual associations between different objects, external or intrapsychic, determined by truth and logical reality, within the 'non-traumatised state'. 'Negative links', on the other hand, such as -K, -L and -H, are associated with 'false communications', as can be observed in projections, like the transference and countertransference which constitute a sort of 'junkyard' of evacuatory processes, such as narcissistic object relations, lies, or false emotions, representing the scaffold that structure the pre-conceptual trauma within the 'traumatised state'. Transference, as well as countertransference, represents false and narcissistic constructs, or negative links, projected into the analyst. They are primeval feelings replicating interactions that took place between the children and their parents, which were then internalised. For instance, 'negative transference' and 'erotic transference' are not 'true hate' or 'true love' (+H and +L), but expressions of fictitious (false) sentiments, or negative links such as -L and -H respectively, which have been displaced and projected. Positive links, on the other hand, are associated with real objects and alpha elements. Negative links block split parts, filling them up with suspicion and distrust, impeding any possibility of integration by preserving a necessary distance, which Klein had already described as essential, between the good and bad objects, thereby impeding any possibility of integration or of achieving the status of total object. An internal traumatised and envious child element could not only attack the capacity to achieve a state of well-being, but could likewise avert the use of creative resources within the self. Also, if projected in the transference, it might flourish as a 'negative therapeutic reaction'. (López-Corvo, 1992, 1995). Positive links, on the other hand, promote integration and assure a change towards total objects and the depressive position, among other issues.

A Clinical Case

A patient who suffered from diabetes would often in the midst of the session, when something relevant was taking place, interrupt the analysis in order to go to the bathroom, as if there existed a direct connection between 'her mind and her bladder'. She was an only child, and once described her parents as being very closed, by joining her hands together as praying. I told her that perhaps she felt very much excluded and very lonely by their closeness, and she agreed.

Her diabetes also became a model to understand how my interpretations symbolised a type of 'food' she would not digest, similar to how sugar in diabetics is not used, and is eventually ousted through the urine. A few months later, when holidays were close, she announced for the first time in four years that she wanted to discontinue her therapy. Around this time, she had a dream that portrayed her deep ambivalence: *was talking to a woman-friend from her book club, about how well she was understanding a book she was reading. Then she was sitting around a*

WHY SELF-ENVY?

long table, like in a convention, but she was sitting on a toilet, and was defecating at the same time as she pretended to be listening to the presenter.

However, during the days that preceded the date of our break, and together with the separation anxiety related to it, new feelings revealed a different use given to discoveries she obtained in her analysis. During one session, for instance, she stated that in the past she thought nothing about what took place in the session; she would usually go to the bathroom, and then drive to a coffee shop where she 'got something sweet in order to get rid of the bitterness of the session'. However, lately she was doing it differently: 'I was thinking about a dream I had yesterday...do you think that there could be more than one interpretation? I really believe that you are the one who appeared in the dream.' And further on: 'Last night I was drawing mandalas[69] from a book and in one of them there was one that looked just like the crater in the dream.'

What I think was relevant in this patient was the new engagement that was taking place during her analysis, even beyond the limits of the session. This was different from before when she would continuously and enviously try to expel my interpretations through her emunctories, or to neutralise with a candy what she felt was a 'bitter criticism'. For the first time a change in attitude was taking place, representing the beginning of a creative 'analytic couple', or the manifestation of a productive link that induced her to continue investigating on her own. It was very interesting to observe that now, when for the first time these changes of attitude were taking place, representing the beginning of a creative 'analytic couple', or the manifestation of a productive link that induced her to continue

---

69 A Hindu or Buddhist graphic of a circle enclosing a square, as a symbol of the universe.

afterwards investigating on her own, was the precise moment when also appeared her desire to leave the analysis.

I wondered if perhaps at the root of her acting-out were inner feelings of self-envy as I have described above; that unconsciously she sensed we were moving to become a 'closer creative couple', possibly similar to how as a child she felt that her parents were. She could have sustained her analysis if the main object was to continue attacking the 'harmonious couple' by not 'digesting' but by defecating and 'sweetening' my interpretations, as she ambivalently had depicted it in her dream. Her ego was attempting to find – through the analysis – a neutral space, or 'alpha function', to deal with the self-envy that she was expressing in her transference, similar to how it was painfully experienced as a child towards her parents when she felt left out. It was a false or negative link that, by being acted out now, served to destroy the help the analysis could have now provided her to contain the pre-conceptual trauma from her past. However, she was instead now attacking, as a false or negative link, the creative relationship she was starting with me, similar to how she also enviously attacked her parents' 'harmonious couple' in the past. It seemed that in her mind she was both the child who enviously attacked her loving parents, and the adult woman she was now, who, similar to her parents, was establishing a creative analytical relationship with me, as if the inner child in her also felt excluded from the new relationship that the thinking, logical inner part of her was now fostering.

I would like to recapitulate what I have previously referred to as self-envy (López-Corvo, 1992, 1994, 1996a, 1999, 2003), representing a condition resulting from an envious interaction between different part-objects, composing the Oedipus structure. I understand that by attempting to facilitate the understanding of the concept of self-envy, or envy between internal parts, I will be facing the risk of repeating myself.

Let us suppose, for instance, that there is an important increment in the amount of envy that a child, who is feeling excluded, experiences towards their parents, and that this envy is mostly directed to what the child acknowledges as feelings of harmony, love, sexuality, creativity, communication, etc., between the couple. As the years go by, these feelings could become idealised and remain in the self as 'foreign' elements not completely assimilated by the ego. When this child grows and becomes an adult, just like his parents were, the envious element that remains unassimilated internally could again be reactivated; but this time, such elements previously envied in his parents are now part of himself.[70] This condition is always reflected in the transference as a sustained attack against idealised links between analyst and patient, experienced as a 'creative', 'productive' and 'harmonious' analytic couple. This situation could either turn into a 'negative therapeutic reaction', or induce a premature disruption of treatment.

Freud and Self-Envy

There are views consistent with the concept of self-envy, produced by Freud in 1932 when he referred to unconscious mechanisms of guilt, which we could now associate with envy between different part-objects in the self. Freud stated:

> I once succeeded in freeing an unmarried woman, no longer young, from the complex of symptoms which had condemned her for some fifteen years to an existence of torment and had

---

70 It is obvious that these interactions take place between internal 'part objects', and not against the self as a totality; in this sense, the term 'self-envy' is not perhaps the most appropriate one; however, beside 'envy between internal part-objects', I have not been able to find a better expression than this one originally used by Scott (1975).

excluded her from any participation in life. She now felt she was well, and she plunged into eager activity, in order to develop her by no means small talent and to snatch a little recognition, enjoyment, and success, late though the moment was. But every one of her attempts ended either with people letting her know or with herself recognizing that she was too old to accomplish anything in that field. After each outcome of this kind a relapse into illness would have been the obvious thing, but she was no longer able to bring that about. Instead, she met each time with an accident which put her out of action for a time and caused her suffering. She fell down and sprained her ankle or hurt her knee, or she injured her hand in something she was doing. When she was made aware of how great her own share might be in these apparent accidents, she, so to say, changed her technique, instead of accidents, indispositions appeared on the same provocations – catarrhs, sore throats, influenza conditions, rheumatic swellings – till at last she made up her mind to resign her attempts and the whole agitation came to an end. (1933, pp. 108–109)

Freud explained the theory behind this conflict as follows:

There is, as we think, no doubt about the origin of this unconscious need for punishment. It behaves like a piece of conscience, like a prolongation of our conscience into the unconscious; and it must have the same origin as conscience and correspond, therefore, to a piece of aggressiveness that has been internalized and taken over by the super-ego. If only the words went together better, we should be justified for all practical purposes in calling it an 'unconscious sense of guilt'. Theoretically, we are in fact in doubt whether we should suppose that all the aggressiveness that has returned from the external world is bound by the super-ego and accordingly turned against the ego, or that a part of it is carrying on its mute and uncanny activity as a free destructive instinct in the ego and the id. A distribution of the latter kind is the more probable; *but we know nothing more about it.*[71] There is no doubt that, when the super-ego was first instituted, in equipping that agency use was made of the piece of the child's aggressiveness towards his parents for which he was unable to effect a discharge outwards on account of his erotic fixation as well as of external difficulties…People in whom this unconscious sense of guilt is excessively strong betray themselves in analytic treatment by the negative therapeutic reaction which is so disagreeable from the prognostic point of view. (ibid, p. 109)

Klein's introduction (1946) of a new architecture of the self, formed by part-object representations, together with primitive defence mechanisms, such as projective and introjective identifications, has established a better perspective to understand the existence within the internal world, of continuous reciprocal part-object interactions. Following this dynamic, Heimann (1952) referred to 'intra-psychic projections' to describe paranoid states:

…but I did not understand how such intra-psychic projection took place, until I came to appreciate the part played by the splitting mechanisms. In the light of Melanie Klein's concept of the paranoid/schizoid position and through her presentation of the defensive processes of splitting in early infantile

---

[71] My italics

life, *I realized that intra-psychic projection is preceded by a split in the ego.*[72] (p. 210)

Rosenfeld (1971) described the existence of a complex destructive mechanism of different part-objects which functions similarly to a 'gang Mafioso'. Joseph (1975) referred to patients 'difficult to reach' in whom splitting of personality induced a resistance of the analysis because one part tries to keep another more needed aspect away from treatment. Grinberg (1976) described the existence of intrapsychic projective identifications directed toward internal objects as a way to explain Freud's dynamics of the lost object in "Mourning and Melancholia". Meltzer (1973) referred to destructive narcissism as a part of the self that presents itself to another suffering good part, 'as a protector from pain, as a servant to its sensuality and vanity and covertly as a brute and torturer'. (p. 97) Steiner (1982) speaks of a 'perverse relationship between different parts of the self' in patients with whom a narcissistic aspect of personality could acquire an exaggerated power and control over healthy parts, inducing them to form a kind of perverse alliance. When the intricacy of these inner relationships is taken into account, 'self-envy' interaction between the representations of different self-parts is quite understandable. (López-Corvo, 1999, pp. 210–211)

'Attack on links that relate', which are revealed in a mind dominated by part-objects instead of total ones, as well as by paranoid-schizoid mechanisms over depressive ones, could be an important way to understand what I have explained above. In this condition, the sense of total object or depressive mechanisms sensed in the external object will induce intense feelings of envy that will result in inner attack of the alpha function, in order to

---

72 My italics.

destroy painful awareness. This destruction will hinder the possibility of achieving the level of total object and, as a result, the closing of a circular behaviour.

Chapter XIII
LONELINESS IN A MAN BORN WITH A DISLOCATED SHOULDER: 'A WILD THOUGHT IN SEARCH OF A THINKER'

I will inculcate over and over, the same counsels to those that over and over commit the same faults.

— Seneca

A baby, quite satisfactorily born, cried and yelled at birth and could not be quieted: the more the mother soothed the child, the more it yelled. It became impossible for the mother to sleep because of this apparently indefatigable yelling.

— Bion, 1994, p. 309

The mind unlearns with difficulty, what is long learned.

— Seneca

Wild Thoughts in Search of a Thinker

Francesca Bion reproduced two tapes recorded by Bion in 1977, which were published twenty years later as a book entitled "Taming Wild Thoughts". The first part discusses the 'Grid', the second one, left untitled, contains what Bion refers to as 'Thoughts without a thinker'. 'If a thought without a thinker comes alone," said Bion, 'it may be what is a stray thought, or it could be a thought with the owner's name...or it could be a wild thought.' Un-thought thoughts can be buried in the profundity of our mind, repressed or forgotten, waiting for a mind to bring them back to life and make proper use of them, similar to Luigi Pirandello's play "Six Characters in Search of an Author". But these 'wild thoughts' could be also dormant in time, never thought of, until a particular thinker finds them, and leaves a mark in history, like Galileo's invention of the telescope or the creation of the telephone by Alexander Graham Bell, among many others. This domain of the unknown, populated by undigested thoughts, has been acknowledged by Bion as the 'beta world', in contrast with the 'alpha function', or capacity to think or digest these beta elements and to provide them with a rational meaning by changing into logical and creative thoughts, or 'alpha elements', which resemble the 'alpha world'.

Bion also mentions, although very slightly, the existence of a mental state unlike those of conscious or unconscious, related to the ineffable, to the presence of the unknown, like primitive events that have taken place very early on in life or during the intrauterine stage. Other researchers, independently of Bion and some even previous to his work, had also referred to the same subject as 'fetal psychic life'; (Raskovsky 1958 and Aray 1992) and also as the 'schizoid secret'. (Lopez-Corvo 1995) In 1976, in relation to these matters, Bion stated:

> After all, if anatomists can say that they detect a vestigial tail, if surgeons likewise can say that they detect tumors which derive from the branchial cleft, then why should there not be what we would call mental vestiges, or archaic elements, which are operative in a way that is alarming and disturbing

because it breaks through the beautiful, calm surface we ordinarily think of as rational, sane behavior? [Bion, 1994, p. 308]

And a year later, the following:

...that besides the conscious and unconscious states of mind, there can be another one. The nearest I can get to giving it a provisional title is the *inaccessible state* of mind. It may become inaccessible because the foetus gets rid of it as soon as it can. Whether it is awareness of its heartbeat, or an awareness of feelings of terror, of sound, or of sight – the kind of sight experienced through the pressure of the optics pits by changes of pressure in the intra-uterine fluid – all that may never have been what we would call either conscious or unconscious. [Bion, 1997, p. 50]

In "Attention and Interpretation" (1970), there is also some allusion to the subject, but in a rather implicit manner if compared with the previous statement which, according to Francesca Bion, was written previously. Being subject to the impact of an 'un-thought thought' could be analogous to, said Bion, '...having a pain without suffering it; not being conscious of a mental phenomenon because it has been repressed; not knowing an event because the event has not occurred'. (1970, p. 11) Or like Christopher Columbus, who believed he had reached the East Indies when in fact he had arrived in America, because he was ignorant of the existence of this continent; or, as Bion once stated about someone not being able to understand the planetary movement, 'because the differential calculus has not been yet invented'.

The reason why we are concerned with happenings from the past that we continuously repeat, but do not remember, is not because of what they were, but because of the mark that was left on us. Bion for instance has assumed that the conclusion of gestation, the fetus, could be aware of unpleasant oscillations in the amniotic fluid as a consequence to conflicts between the parents, or something similar, or could hear voices or loud noises coming from the mother's digestive system, etc. Bion also wondered if, at this level of nearly full-term, the personality might be developed enough as to experience feelings of hostility towards these disturbing things, like 'proto-ideas' or 'proto-feelings' and could split them up, fragment them, and try to evacuate them. He also suggested the existence of certain conditions, which could appear at a given moment, to be so ephemeral, so imperceptible, that we might not even be aware of them, but that could later on become so real that they might even destroy our emotional and peaceful life, without our ever being conscious of it, similar to what Gustav, the patient I will be referring to, painfully experienced through his entire thirty-two years of life. It was quite interesting to observe in this case how a physical hazard at birth later changed into a symbol, and became a powerful emotional restriction.

At the risk of repeating myself, I would like to emphasise what I have already expressed in the first chapter. I have named these kinds of pervasive events as 'pre-conceptual traumas', and considered also that these traumas split the mind in two different dialectical states: the 'traumatised' and the 'non-traumatised'. I have stated too that in practising psychoanalysis, or psychoanalytic psychotherapy, using the notion of the 'pre-conceptual trauma' not only could make procedures much simpler and reduce the time of therapy, but also, and very importantly, could provide a direction to trail. Different from classical therapy, where you usually feel lost, the acknowledgment of the existence of an early and ubiquitous trauma will always provide a bearing that can be followed. After all, pre-conceptual traumas will permanently determine the particular characteristics of any given psychopathology, because it will continuously repeat – repetition compulsion – the same original *meaning*, even if the *actions* of how they might be expressed differs with age. To keep in mind the presence of the pre-conceptual trauma could be similar to resolving a puzzle while using the picture as a guide, instead of doing it blindfolded! All individuals' minds absolutely depend on which mental state will contain which: if the 'traumatised' takes over, the person will unconsciously behave as a confused emotional child, presenting symptoms compatible with the kind of pre-conceptual trauma experienced in childhood. Bion referred to these unconscious repressed elements as 'beta elements'. On the contrary, when the mind is ruled by the 'non-traumatised state' the person will use the 'alpha function' in order to metabolise 'beta elements' – from the 'traumatised state' – and change them into 'alpha elements' which could be used for logical, sensible and creative thinking, according to the individual's age and cognitive development. In simple words, the main purpose of therapy will consist of switching the ruling states from traumatised to non-traumatised. In order to achieve this interchange, the compulsive repetition of the pre-conceptual trauma must be dismantled. However, the 'stickiness of the libido', as Freud referred to it, or the power of magic and omnipotent defences from childhood, are extremely persistent and immensely reluctant to give up; or, in the words of Seneca over 2000 years ago: 'The mind unlearns with difficulty, what is long learned.'

The Man with the Dislocated Shoulder, or 'Wild Thoughts in Search of a Thinker'

Gustav was referred by a psychoanalyst who stated, in a telephone conversation, that after seeing him for around two months, he was unable to understand what exactly was 'wrong with him'. Gustav was a thirty-two year old architect, six years younger than his only brother, who consulted because 'he felt apathetic almost about everything, and did not find any true enjoyment in life'. He emigrated with his family from Turkey when he was ten years of age. He was single and occasionally went out with girls, although he never had a steady girlfriend and was still living with his parents. He mentioned having a girlfriend who was a virgin – something unusual in these times for a twenty-six year old woman – whom he dated several times, before she moved to Australia. I then asked him if he wanted to have a girlfriend in order not to have one.

He often mentioned that he did not experience any emotion, as if he was alexithymic. 'The only time,' he said, 'when I feel happy is when I travel with my friends, otherwise I don't really care.' At one point, when asked what he thought was the reason for not having a steady girlfriend – after all he was a young, single and good looking guy – he stated that it was because he would have to introduce the girl to his parents and he was afraid that they might not like her, and also because he did not wish to hurt her. I then wondered what exactly made him, at his age, be so dependent on his parents. When asked, he denied it, and said that he was not dependent on them, but lived with them for financial reasons. I had the feeling that he feared something, as if he did not trust himself, did not trust his own judgement, and felt that he was still a helpless little boy who was not aware that he had grown up already. It reminded me of what I had referred to in Chapter IV as the 'Onoda syndrome'. I then said that there seemed to be two different parts of him, one that thought and acted like a helpless child, and another as an intelligent, resourceful, and logical adult; however, he will act according to which part of him dominates his mind, whether the child or the adult.

During the first year of analysis, my first impression of him was of someone who acted as if he did 'not exist', was completely dependent on his parents, although terrified of them at the same time, was unable to exercise his own freedom, or possess a project of life and a sense of ownership. At the age of thirty-two he was still acting like an adolescent. I felt unable to produce a logical explanation based on his pre-conceptual trauma, something that could have provided a meaning to his suffering, and remembered the words from the analyst who referred him. I thought that something had happened between him and his parents which was not clear, and insisted telling him that for unknown reasons he seemed to continue treating himself in a manner that he felt his parents had treated him.

At a particular moment, he presented a short dream: *'I have lost my luggage somewhere in South America, and I was wondering if I lost it because I didn't pay the guy to get me my luggage. It wasn't lost but because of regulation, they couldn't give me my luggage.'* He gave no associations and I said that it seemed to me he did not trust others because he feared that the analyst (he knew I was from South America), similar to his apprehension about getting emotionally close to girls, could take something valuable and intimate ('his luggage') from him, because of something he had done ('regulations') and that would leave him completely helpless and totally dependent. After a short pause, he stated that when he was a child his parents travelled often and usually left him with relatives and that his brother, six years his senior, used to bully him; but when he mentioned this to his parents, they did not believe him. He felt that his mother preferred and privileged his brother more than she did him. I then said that I wondered if he felt very lonely, because he felt that he could not trust women, much like how he could not trust his mother, and he did not trust me either, as he possibly felt I was only interested in his money, just as his unconscious appeared to express it in his dream ('he did not pay the guy to get his luggage').

At the next session, he remembered that as a child he was very angry and used to break things, urinate, and defecate everywhere and often locked himself in the bathroom, refusing to get out. I asked what he thought could have been the reason for being so angry. He did not know but remembered that his parents feared he could have become like an uncle who was schizophrenic and who was also very angry. I asked him whether he, as a child, was so angry with his brother and parents that he wished he could kill them but was unable to do so because he was a helpless little boy. Even further, could it be that now, when he had the full agency of an adult, he feared his anger, because now he would be able to inflict harm?

Sometime later, he talked about a girl he was going out with, who had complained about his inability to get emotionally involved with her. I asked him what he thought about this and he answered that most of the time he doesn't care and that this makes no difference to him. I said that perhaps he also was afraid of getting emotionally involved, because, similar to how he felt as a child with his parents in relation to his brother, he feared rejection or abandonment and the feeling that he was not good enough to deserve being loved. Perhaps he was treating himself in a similar way to how he felt his parents had treated him, and feared that everybody, including me, would treat him in a similar manner. He remembered a dream: '*I was in a public bathroom and had to stick my hand in the tub that was full of water in order to get paper towel. Then my gel was overflowing, something that surprised me because I had been using it for a while; then I realized that there were some organisms, like bugs, that continuously reproduced.*' Gustav very seldom offered associations. I said that it seemed to me he wished to make something public (public bathroom) that he also wished to get rid of that 'something', but was not able to do so because he could not clean anything with a 'wet paper towel'. I enquired about what gel he was referring to in his dream, and he answered that it was the cream he used for his face after shaving. I said that the thing he wished to get rid of seemed to 'reproduce' all the time, and I wondered what was this 'thing' that he was referring to, and whether it could be related to his fear of being rejected, as we had previously talked about. At the next session, he presented another dream: *was trying to have a meeting but some of the lights were burned and someone who was there, got angry about that.* I said that it seemed as if he felt disappointed about trying to 'see' something that kept escaping his attention (lights burned) and remained in the darkness.

Two days later, he said that he stayed at his girlfriend 'N''s house for the weekend. He had sex with her but was unable to reach an orgasm even though he tried for quite some time. I said that perhaps he was trying to commit himself emotionally to a relationship with N, but fearing that, he possibly found it difficult to achieve an orgasm. He produced a dream: '*He was biking in a tour with a friend and someone stole their bikes, he became very angry because he did not know how to get back to his place. Then he was trying to climb a mountain but it was very difficult and too dangerous; he finally did it but the video he took was too hazy and it was no good.*' As always he gave no associations and I had the impression that his dreams were like a form of defence, like a 'gift' or a 'distraction' preventing him from saying something. I said that he was ambivalent about his new girlfriend, possibly because this kind of commitment to a girl was something novel for him and it was still frightening, or perhaps because he felt that if he was to get involved, he might not be able to ever free himself (bikes being stolen and not being able to get them back). He is trying to find a way out of his dependency, possibly from his parents and from his childhood, by becoming more independent, but finds it too difficult and dangerous. At the end, he tries to make sense of all of this, but it is too hazy.

At the next session, he revealed something that proved to be critical to his analysis: *he was told by his parents that he was born with a dislocated shoulder*, but he did not remember anything about this. His mother said that after a while they went to the pediatrician, who advised that it was better to wait because it was going to heal by itself. His parents had no recollection at what point the dislocation was discovered, nor how he reacted to it; however, his main difficulty was interrogating his parents, because, as he said, 'he never discusses intimate issues with them'. I said that I was wondering if he may have experienced great pain every time anybody tried to pick him up by pulling his arms, and that perhaps he cried so much that his parents might have felt that he did not like being held or caressed. This could have angered them to the point that they avoided picking him up, and as a result it could have made him feel he was not liked or loved. And it seems that this fear could still be present, to the point that he continues to avoid getting emotionally close to them. He said he did not remember.

Sometime later, he brought a dream similar to the previous one: *he had lost his luggage and was trying to get it but had to look for it in a very difficult terrain.* He said that he had stayed at N's house for the weekend but did not feel very enthusiastic about it, because it made no difference to him whether he was with her or not. As he said this, I felt he talked as if he was proud for not 'having any feelings'. Was this perhaps the way he retaliated due to his parents' indifference for not picking him up? I asked him whether he was dealing with very important emotions that he could not provide meaning to, because they were so primitive and he was unable to remember them much, like how he couldn't remember his dislocated shoulder. And, just like in his dream about the 'public bathroom', his shoulder was like a bug that continuously multiplied and was projected everywhere. He said that he could not get emotionally involved because he always feared that he could end up hurting someone or being hurt himself. I said that he was so convinced that this would happen that he was confusing his own fantasy with reality, feeling that whatever he imagined was actually going to happen; perhaps these feelings were related to his shoulder, something that, although not remembered, was projected everywhere, like a 'memory from the future' *as if he feared that something would happen, which had already happened!* Klein (1959) had stated that

> ...the newborn baby experiences, both in the process of birth and in adjustment to the postnatal situation, anxiety of a persecutory nature. This can be explained by the fact that the young infant, without being able to grasp it intellectually, feels unconsciously every discomfort as though it were inflicted on him by hostile forces. [p. 248]

And also:

> In the earliest stages, love and understanding are expressed through the mother's handling of her baby...The infant's resultant feeling of being understood underlies the first and fundamental relation in his life: the relation to his mother...because in the first few months she represents to the child the whole of the external world, therefore both good and bad come in his mind from her...Both the capacity to love and the sense of persecution have deep roots in the infant's earliest mental processes. [p. 248]

Sometime later he started the session by saying that 'N' had asked him if he could send an email to her sister who lives alone in Seattle, wishing her a happy Christmas. He refused to do it, claiming that he did not know her very well, something that displeased 'N' who then persuaded him to give in. I asked what was so difficult about sending the email, and he stated that 'he does not like this kind of emotional closeness', although he had previously revealed that he had stayed the whole week at N's because his parents were not in town. 'Could it be,' I said, 'that he not only feared becoming emotionally close, but also feared his parents, as though he was still a helpless and dependent little boy?' He then said he does not feel comfortable with 'N' when his parents are at home, but feels free when they are away. When I asked if his parents complained about him having a girlfriend, he said they do not. I then said that he seemed to dread his 'internal parents', much more than he feared the external ones, and to that he agreed. I added that his fear is not only the consequence of powerful and demanding parents in his head, but also that he simultaneously invents himself as a 'helpless little boy'. His combined invention of a 'helpless child' and 'powerful parents' was absolutely disastrous. After a pause, he remembered a dream: *I wanted to go on a trip and I was worried that I had missed something. I had a small school-type bag and I was checking it with my mom to see if I had everything. Then I couldn't find my parking spot. I had to take a train one station up, but couldn't find the door to the parking lot and I was mad because there was not a proper sign.* He offered no associations and I said that the dream seems to be referring to the same subject we were talking about. It appeared that his unconscious was saying that he could not rely on his own judgement and needed his mother or someone else to rescue him: 'he thinks he has lost something,' and I think that he had lost his capacity to trust himself and needed to appeal to his mother to reassure him that everything was fine. He seemed to be angry at me in the transference because I had not provided him with precise directions to find his own 'place', his own identity.

Sometime later, he began the session stating that his girlfriend had just called him to express her gratitude that he had shared details from his work with her. I asked what he meant by that, and he answered that perhaps she liked feeling that he trusted her more if he was revealing aspects of his work. He remembered a dream: *I was in Lebanon – the country where I was born – and I lost my luggage but there wasn't a baggage claim department where I could enquire. I looked among many other pieces of luggage until I found mine and then discovered that the reason why I kept losing it was because I had locked it.* I asked him what he thought was inside his luggage; after all, 'losing his luggage' was a recurring dream. He said he did not know, and then added: 'perhaps my "cojones", or my fear to take chances, or to commit myself'. I said I was wondering if it might be something else, that perhaps what was inside this 'locked luggage' were his 'memories from his dislocated shoulder that he did not wish to remember'. Additionally, since there was not a 'baggage claiming office' at his place of birth where everything had taken place, it could have meant that it was impossible to know where his luggage was, like his broken shoulder, that it is *something that is everywhere, and at the same time, is not*, because it happened at a time when he was too young and could not register it (a pre-conceptual trauma). It is something that he keeps locked or repressed in his mind, not able to recall and at the same time, not wishing to remember.

He started the next session by asking if I knew about an experiment someone had done with monkeys, which were inside a cage that had some bananas hanging from the roof. When one of the monkeys climbed to the top and took them, the rest of the monkeys were punished. As a consequence, the monkeys restrained any monkey who tried to get the bananas from the roof. As the experiment continued, the monkeys were constantly changed for new monkeys, until none of the original monkeys were left. Even though there were none who directly knew that first monkey who took the bananas resulting in the punishment of the others, the group continued restraining monkeys from getting the bananas. It was as if they were continuously doing something without knowing why. I said that the situation in the monkey experiment was similar to what he seemed to be continuously facing: that there is something that terrifies him, that it is very present and everywhere, but that he cannot remember it! He recalled a dream he had on Friday night: *I was presenting an exam in primary school which only consisted of drawing something. I was with a cousin who was also doing the same exam and who in real life used to be a classmate when I was in primary school. At the end, I failed the exam but she passed it.* In another dream, *he is looking for a place to park but fears that he could get a ticket and decided to hide his car. Had to write another exam and had to study in his girlfriend N's books.* He associated these dreams with a conversation he had with 'N' on Friday evening, where she explained that she had too many expenses, and suggested that she sell her car because she does not use it so much. He also thought of moving in with her, but was afraid of telling his parents about it. I said that he feared his independence to do as he wished and felt he had to hide it from his parents (*hiding his car and fearing that he could get a ticket*); also that he feels 'N' is more daring than himself (*he learns from her books*) and he is concerned that 'N' could find out that his fears are like those of a little boy (*primary school*) who fails an easy exam (*drawing anything*) while his cousin (*possibly representing A, because they are from the same country*) succeeds.

The following week, he brought a dream: *the street was flooded and the water level was continuously rising. I got inside of my car to avoid the flood.* Then he continued producing dreams one after the other. I said to him that he was 'flooding us with dreams'. I asked what he thought this dream meant. He said that he did not know, and that I was the one who knew. I said he was bringing dreams and leaving them with me as if they were gifts, but he did not want to get involved. I asked, what he wished to do with so many dreams. He answered that he did not know what to think about them, that it was for me to know. I said that this was true, but they were his dreams and obviously he was closer to them than I was; I could only guess. He answered that he did not know what I meant. I sensed his anger and frustration, possibly as a defence against his fear, and I thought he was bringing dreams because he felt they were important to me, but not to him. He did not wish to get involved, remaining emotionally distant, as he did with 'N' and his parents. I then said that perhaps getting emotionally involved with 'N', his parents or with me, automatically and unconsciously made him relive the terrible pain he might have experienced as a baby, due to his dislocated shoulder. Then he said that 'N' wanted to meet his parents and they wished to meet her too, and this situation was making him feel terrible and very stressed, although he did not know why. 'However,' I said, 'you are the only one who knows why.' But he insisted that he 'did not know, because he doesn't know how to think'. I sensed his anger, although he did not express it, as I tried to help him to think logically in order to contain his unfounded terror that something terrible was going to happen – something which has already happened – if his parents met his girlfriend. However, I sensed he took my enquiry about thinking logically, as a form of attack, and that I was pushing him into a dangerous situation. I thought he was reproducing in his transference what he might have experienced as a baby, when his mother tried to pick him up from his crib in order to lull him, and he then experienced the terrible pain in his shoulder. It must have been like a form of torture she was inflicting on him, something that could have made him extremely angry and frightened.

At the next session, he said that he had arranged a dinner in a restaurant with 'N' and his family. I said that he was very brave to arrange that meeting. He answered that this, however, was not solving the terror that he felt. I then said that the main problem seemed to lie in how difficult it was to remain ignorant about a future that he still did not know, that he ends up convincing himself that whatever he imagined will always happen, as if his fantasy and his reality were the same. Could he consider the possibility that, if in the same manner he imagined the worst, and believed it was going to happen, he could instead imagine something good, and then convince himself that exactly that was going to take place? That this dinner with 'N' and his family, would be something wonderful? It seems that he was always dealing in his mind with 'a memory of the future', when he feared something terrible that was going to happen had already happened. It was like his broken shoulder, that he unconsciously and continuously reproduced in his mind, and then projected everywhere, as something terrible that was going to happen, when in reality, it had already happened.

At the next session, he brought a dream: *I was visiting my friend B's apartment, who is absent, because I wanted to take some paintings I had left with B. There were three pictures, two small and a big one; I decided to take the two small ones and leave the big one.* He gave no associations. I asked about why B was in his dream. He expressed that B was not in his dream. I often have the impression that Gustav has a rather concrete way of thinking, and explained that he is indirectly in his dream because he was 'visiting his apartment'. He said that B was a classmate and a good friend at the University, that he was somewhat a womaniser and not timid like he was. I then asked what he thought were the two small pictures and the big one, and why did he take only the small ones. He said he did not know. 'Could they be B's genitals, his *cojones*, like you often said?' I asked. He laughed and then said: 'Perhaps.' At the next session, he said that, while doing yoga exercises, he was doing the plank and had to hold it for a long time, and 'my left shoulder was in pain, something I never felt before. Perhaps it is my left shoulder that got dislocated.' His complaint reminded me of another patient I had, who went through a very aggressive and painful tonsillectomy when he was a little boy and then, as an adult, he had copious hemorrhages from his throat and nose whenever he faced a stressful situation.[73]

One week after, he said that the dinner with 'N' and his parents went well, but that he was paralysed by fear and 'N' got very angry afterwards because she felt left alone and unsupported. Two weeks later, he announced that his parents had invited 'N' for dinner at their home but he was not as fearful as he had been before. Also, for the first time in his life, he was planning a trip to the Caribbean with 'N', by the end of the month.

Discussion

One difficulty present at the beginning of Gustav's analysis was the predicament of providing a true meaning to his symptoms, to find a reason for his unconscious emotional behaviour, and to visualise the possible anatomy of his pre-conceptual trauma. It was rather challenging to understand what could have justified his feeling of 'not-existence', of not having his own vertex from where he could see the world, as well as his terror at getting emotionally involved and his resistance at finding the reason. At the beginning, I thought about the possibility of a 'diluted' or 'cumulative trauma', like the case of Olga I have previously mentioned in Chapter I. He never got emotionally involved, and he was cautious and evasive. In his dreams, he was always searching for a location where to park, as if he did not have a place of his own, also losing his luggage, possibly representing his identity. He had a desire to be more present but was terrified of attempting to be

---

73 See: López-Corvo (2014, chapter XVI)

so, and was envious of his friends – who often populated his dreams – for being more daring. He often said that travelling with his friend was the only time he felt happy because he then felt free, although I intuited that the sense of freedom he experienced was because of the distance. He found it difficult to get close, and although he attempted to live with his parents he seldom confided with them. He was never late for his sessions, and he never failed to show up, but was always emotionally distant. He had a girlfriend who was virgin and lived in Australia. He acted very passive, attending analysis and expecting to be 'fixed', like an inanimate object, often referring to dreams but using them as a defence to keep a distance, and not showing a true interest in their meaning. He reminded me of the salamander, who lets go of a piece of its tail that wiggles, in order to distract a predator, while it runs and hides. I often experienced in the countertransference an estranged feeling I don't remember having with any patient before, the sensation of dealing with a tragedy that I could never consolidate, as if there was something very important that never made itself present, like the phantom limb of the amputee, like the paradox of an absolute and eternal presence of a total absence! I understood that what he kept losing in his luggage in his dreams was his courage, his 'cojones' as he often said. At one point, while attempting to explain the fear he experienced at approaching his parent, he used 'bungee jumping' as a simile. I said that I could understand the magnitude of his fear when he regarded approaching his parents and jumping with a bungee to be the same thing, and, while I did believe it must be a very frightening experience to jump from a very high bridge tied by your feet with an elastic cord, I did not think that such a jump, and getting emotionally close to his parents or someone else, carried the same emotional impact.

I think Gustav's psychopathology could correspond to what Bion had described as 'an inaccessible mental state', meaning that his terror about getting emotionally close to others, like 'N', his parents or in the transference represented a form of defence or 'emotional anesthesia', often present in individuals who attempt to free themselves from the terror induced by their own emotional dependency. They unconsciously believe that by using projective identification with the purpose of placing their feeling of dependency on others, they will avoid being hurt; a mechanism that is in fact a paradox, because this belief, including the continuous fear of being hurt, is in its totality an invention. None of them are true; they are only unremembered memories from the past that continuously repeat; but acting them out will eventually leave you very frightened as well as completely isolated and lonely! At a particular moment, I said to Gustav that if his compulsive need to remain distant in an attempt to protect himself from being hurt was his own invention, just a fantasy, why couldn't he invent the contrary, that, instead of being hurt, perhaps by getting close to someone he was going to find the opposite: to feel love and be happy! Two sessions later, he brought the answer in a dream! *There was a box in my room containing objects from the past, from the time when I was a child. I opened it and inside were many umbrellas.* I enquired about what he thought the umbrellas meant. 'To protect from the rain,' he answered. 'What rain?' I wondered, and he answered, 'perhaps my crying from my broken shoulder.'

The greatest difficulty in Gustav's analysis was the total absence of references to any memory linked to his dislocated shoulder. The only significant hints we were able to use were his terror around getting emotionally close to anybody, some of his dreams, and Bion's phylogenetic theory of emotional vestiges as a consequence of unregistered events. His intuitive interest about the experiment with monkeys was also a determinant perspective that opened further routes of investigation.

There was a symbolic transformation that I have previously referred to as 'homeomorphic symbolisation',[74] where the expression, form, or behaviour changes but the meaning that supports those changes always remains the same. The terror that he could have experienced when someone pulled him by his arms when he was a baby looks different from his actual terror of intimacy with other persons, including his own parents. However, the emotional meaning behind this action was the same that induced him to fear being picked up when a baby.

Sometime later, he brought a dream: *he was with friends he had invited, in the first class section of an aeroplane from an airline from his country of birth. They were taking off from a field of orange trees, and then he realises that the trees were so close that they were going to damage the engines attached to the wings, so he told the pilot to abort the flight. He wanted to find another flight and went to the counter to change to Lufthansa, but a couple came and cut into the line ahead of him, something he didn't like.* He produced some associations and remembered that his parents used to own an orange orchard in his country when he was a child; also, Lufthansa was a German airline, a country he very much idealised because 'their people were strong and could be trusted'. I said he could have chosen in his dream a proper field to take off from, but he chose his parents' orchard which damaged the engines. Did he have any idea why? He denied this, and I added: 'could the damaged engines represent his dislocated shoulder that he perhaps felt his parents had caused?' Also, it appeared that he was having a good time with friends in first class, and then the

---

[74] I have previously classified symbolisation in two kinds: 'homeomorphic' and 'heteromorphic'.

good time was spoiled by the orange trees, as if he was in his crib having a good time playing by himself with his toys, and then his parents came to pick him up and the good time was spoiled by the excruciating pain from his dislocated shoulder. In his dream, he is trying to escape to Germany, a country he likes, but his parents cut into the line ahead of him. He answered as he often did: 'It is possible but unfortunately I don't remember.' I felt it was difficult to figure out if this dream resulted from interpretations I have provided, or if in fact was a repressed memory from the deep stratus of Bion's *'inaccessible state of mind'*, like a sort of *'wild thought searching for a thinker'*. However, his inhibitions started to change significantly only after the interpretation about the 'dislocated shoulder' being projected everywhere was consistently considered. Shortly after, he presented a dream: *I was invited by someone to board a boat, and as they continued into the open sea, there were many dolphins swimming around the boat that were trying to jump inside the boat to attack me, like trying to take my head off.* He associated this with his fear of being hurt or attacked by others. I said that his dream was reassuring him by possibly telling him the opposite; he could have chosen any fish in his dream, dangerous ones like the sharks, but he chose the most friendly and harmless of all, the dolphins. Could it be that the dream is really telling him that there is in fact nothing to fear?

By the time of this presentation, Gustav announced he was going to be away the upcoming week because he had invited 'N' to go to the Caribbean for the Easter break. He looked unusually pleased. I asked if he had ever invited a girl to go away for a holiday, and he answered with a smile: 'never'. In any case his analysis continues.

REFERENCES

Aktar, S. and O'Neil, M. K. Hopelessness. London: Karnac Books.
Anthony, E. J. (1956). The Significance of Jean Piaget for Child Psychiatry. J. Med. Psychol., 29, 20–34.
Anzie, D. (1986). Beckett et Bion. Revue de Psychothérapie Psychanalytique de Groupe, 5–6: 286.
Aray, J. (1992). *Momentos psicoanalíticos*. Caracas: Monte Avila Editors.
Bair, D. (1978). A Biography, Samuel Beckett. New York: Harcourt Brace Jovanovich.
Bawlf, S. (2003). The Secret Voyage of Sir Francis Drake. Vancouver: Douglas & McIntyre.
Bick, E. (1968). The experience of the skin in early object relations. Int. J. of Psychoanal. 49, pp. 484–6.
Bion W. R. (1948). Experience in Groups. London: Tavistock, 1961.
____ (1957). Differentiation of the psychotic from the non-psychotic personalities, in *Second thoughts*. New York: Jason Aronson, 1967.
____ (1959). Attacks on linking, in *Second thoughts*. London: Karnac Books.
____ (1962). Learning from Experience. London: Karnac Books, 1984.
____ (1963). Elements of Psycho-Analysis, in *Seven servants*. London: Karnac Books, 1984.
____ (1965). Transformations, in *Seven servants*. London: Karnac Books.
____ (1967). Second Thoughts, Selected Papers on Psychoanalysis. London: Karnac Books, 1993.
____ (1970). Attention and interpretation. London: Karnac Books, 1984.
____ (1974). *Brazilian lectures*, Sao Paulo No 1, Río de Janeiro: Imago Editora Ltda.
____ (1976). On Quotation from Freud, in *Clinical Seminars and Four Papers*. Oxford: Fleetwood Press, 1987.
____ (1977). *Seven Servants*. London: Karnac Books.
____ (1987). Clinical Seminars and other Works. London: Karnac Books, (1994).

____ (1992). *Cogitations*. London: Karnac Books.
____ (1994). Clinical seminars and other works. London: Karnac Books.
____ (1997). Taming Wild Thoughts. London: Karnac Books,
Bleándonu, G. (1994). Wilfred Bion. His Life and Works 1897–1979. London: Free Association Books.
Boris H. N. (1976). On Hope: Its Nature and Psychotherapy. Int. J. Psychoanal. 3: 139–150.
Bowlby, J. (1980). *Loss: Sadness & depression. Attachment and loss* (vol. 3); (International psycho-analytical library no.109). London: Hogarth Press.
Bowlby, J. (1988). Attachment, communication, and the therapeutic process. *A secure base: Parent–child attachment and healthy human development*, 137–157.
Cohn, R. (1967). Case book on Waiting for Godot. New York: Grove Press, Inc.
Cormier, R. and Pallister, J. L. (1979). Waiting for Death. Alabama: University of Alabama Press.
De Saint-Exupéry, A. (1943). The Little Prince. Kentauron. Kindle Edition.
Deutch, H. (1942). Some forms of Emotional Disturbance and their Relationship to Schizophrenia. Psychoanalytic Quarterly, 6. 11: 301–321.
Fairbairn, W. R. D. (1952). *Psychoanalytic Studies of the Personality.* London: Routledge & Kegan Paul.
Ferenczi, S. (1949). Confusion of the Tongues between the Adults and the Child. Int. J. Psycho-anal. 30: 225–230.
Freud, S. (1905). Three Essays, *Three Essays on the Theory of Sexuality.* SE, Vol. VII. London: Hogarth Press.
____ (1914). Remembering, Repeating and Working Through. SE, Vol. XII. p. 215.
____ (1927). The Future of an Illusion, SE, Vol. XXI. London: Hogarth Press.
____ (1933). New Introductory Lectures on Psycho-Analysis. Lectures XXIX–XXXV. SE, Vol. XXII.
Girzone, J. F. (1989). Foreword. In *Saint Francis of Assisi,* Chesterton, G.K. New York: Doubleday.
Green, A. (2002). Time in Psychoanalysis. London: Free Association Books.
Grinberg, L. (1976). Teoría de la Identificación. Buenos Aires: Editorial Paidós.

REFERENCES

Grosskurth, P. (1986). Melanie Klein, her World and her Work. Toronto: McClelland & Stewart Ltd.

Harlow, H. F. (1958). The nature of love. *American Psychologist, 13,* 673–685.

Harvey, M. (2008). Painter in a Savage Land. New York: Random House.

Heimann, P. (1952). Preliminary Notes on some Defence Mechanisms in Paranoid States. Int. J. Psychoanal. 33: 208–203.

Hendrick, I. (1942). Instinct and the Ego during Infancy. Psychoanal. Quarterly. Pp. 11, 33–58.

Joseph, B. (1975). The patient who is difficult to reach. In Tactics and Techniques in Psychoanalytic Therapy. Vol. 2, Countertransference, ed. Giovacchini, P. L. pp. 205–216. New York: Jason Aronson.

Kanner L. (1943). Autistic disturbances of affective contact. *Nervous Child.* 2, 217–250.

Khan, M. (1963). The Concept of Cumulative Trauma. *Psychoanal. Study of the Child.* 18: 286–306.

Klein, M. (1946). Notes on Some Schizoid Mechanisms. In: *Envy and Gratitude.* London: Hogarth Press. 1975. Publications, Reprint, New York, 1971.

_____ (1959). Our Adult World and Its Roots in Infancy, 1959. In: *Envy and Gratitude and Other Works.* New York: The Free Press, 1975.

_____ (1963). On the Sense of Loneliness. In: *Envy and Gratitude and Other Works.* New York: The Free Press, 1975.

Knowlson, J. (1996). Damned to Fame: The Life of Samuel Beckett. New York: Grove Press.

Laplanche, J. and Pontalis, J. B. (1967). The Language of Psychoanalysis. London: Karnac Books. 1988.

López-Corvo, R.E. (1977). God is a Woman. New York: Jason Aronson.

_____ (1980). Símbolo y Mutación. Caracas: Monte Avila.

_____ (1992). About Interpretation of Self-Envy. Int. J. Psychoanal. 73:719–728.

_____ (1993). A Kleinian Understanding of Addiction. In: *M. Klein and Object Relation Journal, Vol. 11, No 1.*

_____ (1995). Self-envy, Therapy and the Divided Inner World. Northvale, NJ: Jason Aronson.

_____ (1999). Self-envy and Intrapsychic Interpretation, *Psychoanal. Quarterly, Vol. LXVII, No 2.*

_____ (2003). The Dictionary of the Work of W. R. Bion. London: Karnac Books.

_____ (2006). The Forgotten Self, with the use of Bion's Theory of Negative Links. *Psychoanal. Review.* 93: 363–377.

_____ (2006a). Wild Thoughts Searching for a Thinker, a Clinical Application of W. R. Bion's Theories. London: Karnac Books.

_____ (2013). The distortion between "Conceptual" and "Pre-conceptual" traumas. *Psychoanal. Review.* 100 (2), April.

_____ (2014). Traumatized and Non-traumatized States of the Personality. London: Karnac Books.

_____ (2017). La Trampa Traumàtica: Quan estar sortint significa que s'està entrant! Revista Catalana de Psicoanàlisi. Vol. XXXIV/2.

Mahler, M. (1972). On the First Three Sub Phases of the Separation-Individuation Process. In *Select Papers*, New York: Jason Aronson, vol. 2.

Meltzer, D. (1966). The Relation of Anal Masturbation to Projective Identification. Int. J. Psychoanal. 47: 335–342.

_____ (1967). The Psychoanalytic Process. London: Heinemann.

_____ (1973). Sexual States of the Mind. London: Clunie Press.

_____ Bremner, J., Hoxter, S., et al. (1975). Exploration in Autism. Perthshire, Scotland: Clunie Press.

_____ (1978). The Kleinian Development Part III, *The Clinical Significance of the Work of Bion.* Perthshire, Scotland: Clunie Press.

_____ (1984). Dream-Life, A Re-examination of the Psycho-Analytical Theory and Technique. Scotland: Clunie Press.

_____ (1986). Studies in Extended Metapsychology: Clinical Application of Bion's ideas. London: Clunie Press.

_____ (1992). The Claustrum: An investigation of claustrophobic phenomena. London: Clunie Press.

Miller, I. (2013). Beckett and Bion. London: Karnac Books.

Paz, O. (1997). El Laberinto de la Soledad y otras Obras. New York: Penguin Books.

Peplau, L. A. and Perlman, D. (1982). Perspectives on loneliness. In L.A. Peplau & D. Perlman, (Eds.). Loneliness: *A sourcebook of current theory, research, and therapy.* (pp. 1–18). New York: Wiley-Interscience.

Pérez Morazzani, A. M. and López-Corvo, R. E. (2017). The Essential Being. London: Karnac Books.

REFERENCES

Piaget, J. (1961). La Formación del Símbolo en el Niño. México: Fondo de Cultura Económica.

―――― (1962). Play, Dream and Imitation in Childhood. New York: W. W. Norton & Company Inc.

―――― (1965). La Construcción de lo Real en el Niño. Buenos Aires: Edit. Proteo.

Pontamianou, A. (1997). Hope. A Shield in the Economy of Borderline States. London: Routledge.

Rosenfeld, H. (1971). A Clinical Approach to the Psychoanalytic Theory of Life and Death Instincts. Int. J. Psychoanal. 52:169.

Rotenberg, K. J. and Hymel, S. (1999). Loneliness in Childhood and Adolescence. Cambridge: Cambridge University Press.

Sartre, J. P. (1950). Baudelaire. New York: New Direction Books.

Scott, W. C. M. (1975). Self-Envy and Envy of Dreams and Dreaming. International Review of Psycho-Analysis 2: 333.

Sohn, L. (1985). Narcissistic Organization, Projective Identification and the Formation of the Identificate. Int. J. Psychoanal. 66: 201–214.

Spitz, R. A. (1945). Hospitalism: An Inquiry into the Genesis of Psychiatric Conditions in Early Childhood. *The Psychoanalytic Study of the Child*, 1, 53–74.

Steiner, J. (1982). Perverse Relationships between Parts of the Self: A Clinical Illustration. *Internat. J. of Psychoanal.* 63: 241–2.

Stevens, V. (2005). Nothingness, Nothing, and Nothing in the Work of Wilfred Bion and in Samuel Beckett's Murphy. *Psychoanal. Rev.*, 92: 607–635.

Taylor, G. J., Bagby, R.M. and Parker, J.D.A. (1997). Disorders of Affect Regulation: Alexithymia in Medical and Psychiatric Illness. UK: Cambridge University Press.

Tobias, N. C. (2017). Jewish Conscience of the Church: Jules Isaac and the Second Vatican Council. Cham, Switzerland: Pelgrave Macmillan.

Unamuno, M. De. (1954). The Tragic Sense of Life. New York: Dover Publications Inc.

Weiss, R. S. (1973). Loneliness: The experience of Emotional and Social Isolation. Cambridge, MA: Mit Press.

Whitman W. (1855). Leaves of Grass. New York: Dover Publications Inc. 2007.

REFERENCES

Winnicott, D. W. (1958). The Capacity to be Alone. In *The Maturational Processes and the Facilitating Environment: Studies in the Theory of Emotional Development.* London: Karnac Books, 1965.

INDEX

A

Abandoned element, 161
Abandonment, 81, 104, 128, 161, 187
Absence of a thing, 112
Absent breast, 154
Abuse, 165
Accuser, 165
Acting out, 24, 72
Acting out perverse, 93
Addiction, 124
  – drug, 117
  – marijuana, 117
Adultisation, xix, 48
Aggression, 13, 17, 35, 42, 50, 51, 58, 149
  – childhood, 13
  – child's, xviii, 56
  – drive, 162
  – libido, 53
  – parental, 152
  – passive, 152
  – unconscious guilt and, 162
Aggressiveness, 176
Aloneness, 10, 63, 65, 133, 134, 150
Alpha elements, 3, 38, 44. *See also* Bion, Wilfred
Alpha function, xxii, 3, 11–15, 17, 23, 44, 54, 72, 109, 125, 166, 169. *See also* Bion, Wilfred
  – analyst's, 21
  – attack on, 178
  – beta elements, 6
  – simple logic and, xxiii
  – thinking capacity, 170

Ambivalence, 19, 20, 51, 58, 81, 93, 98, 102, 107, 123
  – adolescent, 125
  – borderline structure and, 116
  – extreme form of, 115
Anal claustrum, 117
Analytic couple, 96n41, 173, 175
Anxiety, viii, xvi, 12, 15, 18, 29, 71, 93, 157, 162, 163
  – bouts of, 82
  – castration, 74
  – children's, 128
  – chronic, 151
  – complete absence of, 32
  – ego-inducing, 167
  – guilt-ridden, 157
  – retaliatory, 167
  – weaning, 118
Aristarchus of Samos, 32
Aristotle, 32
As-if personality, xix
Autistic psychosis, 152
Autonomy, 63, 111, 112, 125

B

Bad object, 167
Basic assumptions, 4, 136. *See also* Bion, Wilfred
  – dependence, 136, 137
  – fight-flight, 136
  – pairing, 136
Basic delusion, 101, 102, 106
Baudelaire, Charles Pierre, 79, 115, 120–124

INDEX

Becket, Samuel, 138–151
- Bion and, 148

Bereavement, 149

Beta elements, xxiii, 3, 5, 10–14, 44, 48, 53, 129. *See also Bion, Wilfred*

Bick, Esther, 48, 50

Biological absence, 106

Bion, Francesca, 182

Bion, Wilfred, vii, xi, xxii, 1–6, 13, 23, 33, 38, 48, 90, 91, 95, 138, 164, 170. *See also Alpha function, Beta elements, Negative links, Positive links and Thinking.*
- alpha function, 6, 129, 133, 184
- animate and inanimate, 34
- beta elements 70, 109, 184
- binocular vision, 109
- digestion, 6
- emotional vestiges, 198
- hallucinations, 55
- human and material objects, 35
- inaccessible state of mind, 182, 198, 200
- links, 150
- maternal reverie, 89
- narcissistic, 130, 133
- pre-conceptions, 53
- proto-feelings, 183
- proto-ideas, 183
- psychotic and non-psychotic states, 5
- reversible perspective, 171
- social-istic, 130, 133
- theory of thinking, 1, 21, 56
- truth, 31
- wild thoughts, 181

Boundary, 50, 64

Bowlby, John, x

C

Castration, 101, 106, 157
- anxiety, 101, 115, 158
- repetition compulsion, 56
- retaliatory, 99

Child-faecal-penis, 114, 115. *See also Mental space*

Claustrum, 67, 87, 88, 113, 114
- genital, 113
- head/breast, 113
- maternal rectum, 113, 116, 117

Cognition, 4

Communication, 23

Conceptual trauma, 3, 7

Conflict, 9, 12, 15, 25, 47, 69, 74, 128, 147
- ambivalent emotions, 79
- nature of, 81
- non-existence and, 133
- Oedipal, 73, 92, 155
- unconscious need for punishment, 176

Confrontational discussants, 133

Confusing breast, 168

Confusion, viii, 24–27, 29, 30, 36, 115

Consciousness, viii

Constant conjunction, 3n10, 53

Countertransference, 9, 10, 45–48, 68, 76
- feeling trapped, 118
- projections and, 171
- transference and, 157

Creative couple, 174

Creativity, 92

Cumulative trauma, 8

D

Dasein, 63, 150
- relation to oneself, 134, 135

INDEX

Death instinct, 92
Death terror of, 148
Defence, 72
- against fear, 194
- catastrophic change, 16
- form of, 45, 154, 198
- homosexuality, 18
- idealisation, 151
- masochistic, 99
- mechanism, xiii, 157
- omnipotent, 14, 15, 20, 21, 26, 59
- powerlessness and, 33

Denial, xvi, 71, 94, 105
Dependency, xxii, 63, 111, 147
- alexithymia and, 34
- emotional, 74, 117
- fear of, 24, 26, 33, 34
- gender related, 34
- pre-conceptual trauma and, 34
- shameful weakness, 34

Depression, viii, xvi, 18, 74, 93
- bouts of, 37, 67

Depressive position, 92, 93n39, 172
Despair, xvi, 56, 71, 75, 88, 88n35, 134
Deutsch, Helene, 48
Differentiation, 31, 50
Disavowal, 13, 106
Disequilibrium, 124
Dissociated states, 116
Dissociation, 58
Dream furniture, 70. *See also Bion, Wilfred*
Drive, xxii, 58, 84, 99, 111, 161, 162, 173. *See also Freedom drive*

E

Ego, 72, 81, 82, 157, 167
- alpha function and, 174
- aptitude of, 95
- aspect of, 105
- child, 158
- destructive instinct and, 177
- ideal, 73
- observing, 76
- polarisation of, 58
- pre-conceptual trauma and, 81
- Psychology, 91
- rebelling, 81
- representing child, 164

Egocentrism, 24, 32
Emotional anaesthesia, 198
Emotional entanglement, xviii
Emotional loneliness, x, xi
Emotional needs, 34
Emotional trap, 69
Emotions, xviii, xix, 9, 34, 44, 45, 58, 59, 63, 116, 129, 136, 149, 151, 165
- ambivalent, 79
- cognition and, 5
- early situations and, 43
- false, 171
- Klein's psychology, 4
- repressed, 3
- split, 78
- trauma structure and, 11

Emotions unconscious, 5
Empty plenitude, 114, 123. *See also Faecal penis*
Enforced splitting, 35 n21
Envy, 63, 69, 75, 132
- feeling excluded, 175
- intense feelings, 178
- internal, 165
- introjection, 166
- murderous, 131
- Oedipal, 73
- original, 99
- phallic, 72, 101, 152, 156, 158

[209]

INDEX

- presence of, 133
- private longing, 166
- projection of, 166
- splitting, 166
- superego and, 167
- trail of, 23–25
- undescriptive, 102

Epistemology, vii, ix, xvi, 5, 10, 15, 40
Erotic fixation, 177
Exclusion, 62, 78, 101, 105, 157
- feelings of, 161
- Oedipus, 74
- projected, 78, 101
- function of, 132

Existentialism, 86

F

Faeces, 161
- degrading to, 115
- idealisation of, 114

Fairbairn, Ronald, 53, 91
False-self, 17
Father, 112
- absence of, 46, 55, 67, 111, 112, 116, 117, 119–125, 159, 162
- Beckett's, 143–149
- figure, 48
- independence and freedom, 89
- mother's narcissistic absence and, 106
- murdered internal, 17
- need for, 102
- neutralising mother, 87, 88, 112
- Oedipal, 98, 115, 155, 156
- powerful, 60
- punitive, 95
- rescuer, 98

Faustian sacrifice, 99
Faecal penis, 114. *See also Faecal phallus*
Faecal phallus, 106, 111, 116, 120, 125. *See also Faecal penis*
Ferenczi, Sandor, 70, 79, 90, 135
Foetal psychic life, 181
Formal operations, 162
Freedom, 112, 117
- absolute, 64
- drive, 111, 113
- sense of, xxii

Freud, Ana, 137
Freud, Sigmund, xxiii, 2, 29, 36, 37, 52–54, 72, 92, 114, 147, 155, 160, 161
- cloacae theory, 115
- ego ideal, 167
- protective shield, 89
- theory of instinct, 53
- unconscious need for punishment, 176

Frustration, 52, 55–57, 94, 95, 107, 168, 194

G

Gaia, 111
Gang Mafioso, 178. *See also Rosenfeld, Herbert*
Generalisation, 36
Geocentric theory, 32
Ghosts, 70, 78
Good object, 167
Grinberg, Leon, 178
Growth, 44, 63, 87, 109, 112, 113
Guilt, 12, 20, 58, 59, 93, 148, 165
- child's, 167
- extreme, 121
- feeling of, 99
- masochistic, 106
- unconscious, 63, 95, 162
- unconscious mechanisms of, 175

H

- unconscious sense of, 176, 177
- vomit, 169

Hate, 14, 102, 136. *See also Negative links and Positive links*
Heidegger, 63, 85, 134, 135, 150
Heimann, Paola, 177
Heliocentric theory, 32
Helplessness, xiii, 7, 15, 20, 41, 45, 57, 65, 74, 259, 165
- Oedipus Complex and, 62
- sense of, xvi, 60, 139
- sensed biological, 26

Heterophobia, 119
Homeomorphic symbolisation, 199
Hope, 85
- by renunciation, 10, 94, 106
- defensive aspect, 94
- false, 100
- Hesiod's, 86
- historical, 84
- metapsychology, 92
- narcissistic, 86
- non-traumatised state, 92
- pathological, 92
- psychoanalysis, 91
- purpose, 92
- vengeful, 10, 93, 105, 106

Hume, David, 3n10

I

Idealisation, 8, 73n31, 105, 114, 116, 151, 165, 167
Identificate, 72, 93. *See also Sohn, Leslie*
Identification, 48, 87, 112
- cultural or biological, 155
- mutual, 158
- parental, 156
- process of, 157, 164
- projective and introjective, 157
- with aggressor, 137

Image parental, 158
Imitation, xiii, 48, 157
- chameleonic, 48
- contemplative, 49
- differed, 48
- immediate, 48, 49

Impasse, 25
Impotence, xiii, xix, 8, 15, 24, 26, 99, 159, 161
Impulse theory, 92
Inclusion, 78, 101, 105, 106
- place of, 89, 90

Independence, 63, 64, 89, 111, 117, 125, 131, 147, 169, 193
Internal and external reality, 30
Internal loneliness, xi
Internal representations, 48
Interpretation, 13, 25, 33, 39, 57–59, 76, 81, 95, 132
- alpha function and, 17
- extra-transferencial, 25
- form of, 25
- intrapsychic, 25
- introducing integration, 16
- transferencial, 25

Intimacy, 199
Introjection, 25, 50, 87, 112, 166, 167
Introjective identification *See also projective identification*, 19, 33, 44, 45, 74, 79, 82

J

Jealousy, xviii, 28

INDEX

K

Khan, Massud, xv
Klein, Melanie, 4, 23, 43, 53, 165, 172, 177, 190
Kronos, 111

L

Libido, 53, 91, 184
Libido stickiness, 184
Lies, 70, 171
Links, 83, 173. *See also Negative links and Positive links*
Logical thinking, 13, 54
Love, 64, 90, 98, 175, 198
– aloneness and, 65
– coming from the breast, 35
– erotic transference and, 171
– father's, 107
– mother's handling of baby, 190
– need and, 64
– sex and, 103
– unconditional, 47, 87, 89, 111, 147

M

Magical thinking, 14
Masochism, 26, 121, 137, 151
Maternal power, 88
Maturation process, 113, 114
Meaning, 37, 91, 131, 138, 181, 184, 186, 199
– hidden, 112, 157
– internal objects and, 36
– narcissistic, xi, 130, 131, 134. *See also Bion, Wilfred*
– pre-conceptual trauma, xxii, 21
– repetition compulsion, 54
– sense of, 130
– social-istic, 131

– source of, 130
– unconscious, 9, 36
Meltzer, Donald, 4, 5, 48, 53, 67, 87, 93, 94, 114, 169, 178
– faecal phallus, 117
– mother's anal claustrum, 116
Memory from the future, 190
Mental apparatus, 38
Mental logic, 10
Mental pain, 109
Mental space, 87, 112, 116. *See also Space*
Mental trap, 15, 21
Mother, 18, 28, 160, 180
– abandoning, 69
– absence of, 7, 90, 105
– anal claustrum, 116
– breast-faeces-baby, 115
– dyadic, 101
– excess of, 67, 111–125
– first object choice, 156
– internal malignant, 56
– loving, x
– narcissistic injury and, 101
– narcissistic symbiosis, 125
– part, 82
– phallic, 106
– presence of, 9, 116
– projected, 12
– refrigerator, 153
– total presence of, 116
– unconditional love and, 89
Mother-breast-faeces-baby, 115

N

Nameless fear, 24
Nameless terror, 105
Narcissism, 92
– destructive, 178

- normal, 10, 134
- pathological, 10, 134
- primary, 33
- secondary, 53

Narcissistic absence, 101, 117, 153, 161
Narcissistic equilibrium, 17
Narcissistic fusion, 106
Narcissistic injury, 101
Narcissistic structure, 35, 40, 94
Narcissistic symbiosis, 117
Need, 64, 102
Neediness, 63
Negative links, 170–174. *See also Links and Positive links*
- minus hate (–H), 170
- minus knowledge (–K), 170, 171
- minus love (–L), 171

Negative therapeutic reaction, 75, 132, 172, 175, 177
Nietzsche, Friedrich, 85
Non-existence, 41, 126, 130, 196
- Bion, Wilfred, 131
- feelings of, 133

Non-traumatised state, viii, xix, xx, xxii, 3–5, 8, 11–16, 21, 37, 64, 65, 71, 76, 96, 105, 108, 134, 153, 183. *See also Traumatised state*
- cognitive progression, 129
- contain traumatised state, 109
- control, 83
- creativity, 94
- dialectic struggle, 129
- hope and, 94
- normal narcissism, 134
- paralysed, 129
- positive links and, 171
- reparation, 94
- repetition compulsion, 54

No-things, 78

O

Object
- absence of, 7
- choice, 156
- containing, 50
- dead, 114
- desire, 161
- external, 50, 178
- idealised, 167
- internal, 36, 38
- lost, 102, 107, 178
- malignant, 114
- non-existent, 132
- primary, 7, 107, 109
- projective-identification-rejecting, 38
- relations, 91
- relations narcissistic, 92
- revengeful idealised, 165
- revengeful internal, 114
- total, 178, 179
- transitional, 36
- univalent total, 16
- projected bizarre, 70

Obsessive autistic detachment, 153
Oedipal conflict, 73
Oedipus complex, vii, 89, 102, 155, 158, 160
- Oedipus negative, 48, 156
- Oedipus positive, 156

Oedipus structure, 174
Oedipus trap, 87
Omnipotence, xiii, 24, 26, 57. *See also Impotence*
Omnipotent control, 107
Omniscience, 23, 57
Onoda, 71
Onoda syndrome, 70, 96, 185

[213]

INDEX

Ortega y Gasset, 65
Osho, 34

P

Pandora's box, 88
Paranoia, 24, 26, 30, 32, 33, 45
Paranoid-schizoid position, 78, 92, 167, 177
Parental imagoes, 93
Part-object, 78
– bivalent, 78
– different, 174, 178
– internal , 132
– internalised ego, 132
– representations, 177
– reproduce, 82
– superego internal, 132
Paz, Octavio, vii, viii
Penis, 31, 60, 103, 125, 160, *See also Phallus*
– artificial, 119
– biological absence and, 106
– breast, 118
– fabricated, 120
– faecal, 114
– idealised, 170
– imaginary, 115
– knowledge, 169
– lacking, 156
– narcissistic absence and, 101, 102, 117
– steal, 168
Permanent presence, 7
Persecution, 82, 167, 190
Perversion, 160, 161
Phallus, 124, *See also Penis and Faecal Phallus*
– denigration of, 116
– idealisation of, 116

– symbol and, 87
Phantasy, 29, 111
– masturbatory, 119
– mother's, 114
– sadistic, 170
Piaget, Jean, xxii, 4, 5, 36, 46–49
– formal operations, xxiii
– imitation, 48
– imitation differed, 48
– imitation immediate, 48, 49
– imitation representative, 48
Pirandello, 71
Plato, 1, 6, 70
Positive links, 171, 172
Powerlessness, 33, 96, 165
Pre-conceptual trauma, viii, xiv, xix, xxii, xxiii, 2, 4, 8, 9, 11, 33, 44, 52–57, 62, 65, 77, 95, 96, 103, 107, 109, 128, 129, 139, 151, 156–163
– anatomy of, 196
– Baudelaire, 123
– constant conjunctions, 3
– control of, 81
– core of, 69, 170
– dynamics of, 164
– meaning, 186
– parasites, 2
– pervasive events, 183
– presence of, 184
– source of, 79
– specific emotions, 78
– structure, 72, 113, 171
– traumatised state and, 71
– unconscious repetition, 3
– universal, 7
Present-absences, 78, 89
Primary deprivation, x
Projection, 24, 30, 165
– form of, 166

INDEX

- intra-psychic, 177
- two part objects, 167

Projective and introjective identification, 19, 33, 44, 45, 48, 71, 74, 79, 82, 134, 157, 177

Projective identification, 14, 18, 20, 23, 25, 34, 44, 45, 74, 75, 76, 79, 82, 158, 198
- self-flagellation, 82

Prometheus, 88

Pseudo-adult, xix

Psychogenic autism, 152, 153

Psychopathology, vii, xv, xxii, 2, 5, 9, 15–17, 44, 54, 63, 71, 94, 97, 157, 183

Punishment, xiii, xv, 27, 35, 99, 121, 192
- masochistic need for, 93, 95, 167
- need for, 137, 149, 162, 176
- Tantalus, 108

R

Regression, 63, 94

Relationship
- one-body, xi
- two- and three-body, xi

Renunciation hope, 84

Reparation, 92, 94, 95

Repetition compulsion, viii, 2, 6, 16, 29, 52, 53, 57, 156
- logical thinking, 54
- meaning, 184
- primitive defence, 56

Representation, 79, 87, 112
- internal, 158

Rescuer, 13, 24, 64, 81, 98, 126, 127, 150–153, 155, 158, 165
- Bion's basic assumptions and, 136
- common, 135
- outside, 134

Rescuer-placer, 66

Resistance, 21, 94, 109, 178, 196

Retreat, 94, 100

Reverie, 2, 7

Rosenfeld, Herbert, 178

S

Saint-Exupery, x, xx, xxi, 40, 65

Sartre, 85, 121

Schizoid secret, 153, 181

School phobias, 128, 162

Second opportunity, 21

Secondary skin, 50

Selected fact, 16, 89. See also Bion, Wilfred

Self, xi, 10, 30, 32, 50, 53, 94, 164, 172, 175, 177, 178

Self-castration, 117

Self-confidence, 29

Self-devaluation, 72

Self-envy, 13, 14, 25, 45, 57, 63, 96, 106, 115, 121, 129–133, 164, 178
- between parts, 165
- between parts, 168
- feelings of, 174
- form of, 132, 169
- Freud, Sigmund and, 175
- mechanisms, 75
- negative links and, 170
- prevalent, 166

Self-flagellation, 137

Selfness, 63

Sense-data, 38

Separation, x, 118, 128, 162
- anxiety, xxiii, 173

Sex addiction, 102

Sibling rivalry, 12, 101, 119

Signal theory, 29

Signs and symbols, 112

[215]

INDEX

Sisyphus complex, 116
Social loneliness, x
Sohn, Leslie, 72, 93
Space, 2, 10, 16, 52, 87, 119, 134
 – concept of, 50
 – genital claustrum, 114
 – mental, 87, 112, 116
 – neutral, 174
 – Oedipus complex and, 161
Spitz, Rene, x
Splitting, 24, 58, 92, 166, 177, 178
 – defensive process of, 177
 – enforced, 35
 – personality, 178
Steiner, John, 93
Stickiness of the libido, 184
Stockholm syndrome, 81
Superego, 26, 72, 81–83, 157, 158, 164, 167, 176, 177
 – cruel, 58
 – first instituted, 177
 – kidnapper, 81
 – narcissistic structure, 73
 – sadistic, 25, 75
 – taming, 81
 – threat, 74
Symbiotic psychosis, 152
Symbol, 87, 112, 183
Symbol formation, 113
Symbolisation, 10, 16, 36, 87, 112, 113
 – heteromorphic, 37
 – homeomorphic, 37
Symptom, 8, 29, 78

T

Thinking, 44, 109, 184, 195
 – children's, 5, 23, 33, 36, 44, 46, 48
 – logical, 12–15, 54, 56, 94, 194
 – magical, 14, 94

 – symbolical, 4
 – theory of, 1, 21, 56. *See also Bion, Wilfred*
 – toxic, 109
 – zero-sum form of, 23, 25
Time, 16
Total perfection, 24
Toxic thinking, 109
Transductive logic, 10
Transference, 9, 10, 19, 32, 37, 43–48, 58, 59, 80, 132, 134, 166, 171
 – countertransference interaction, 47, 67. 72, 82
 – disappointment, 74
 – erotic, 171
 – negative, 171
 – perversion of, 169
 – reciprocal link, 157
 – superego and, 79
Trauma *See also Traumatised state and Non-traumatised state*
 – containing, 22
 – cumulative, xv, 196
 – entanglement, xvi, 3, 45, 57
 – pre-conceptual, xv
 – psychic, 89, 90
 – ubiquitous, xv
Traumatic path, 83
Traumatic trap, 70
Traumatised state, viii, xii, xix, xx, 3–5, 12, 13, 16, 17, 28, 36, 38, 43, 44, 64, 65, 70, 71, 105–108, 133, 134, 153, 183. *See also Non-traumatised State*
 – available, 165
 – childlike emotional performances, 23
 – contain, 125
 – emotional confusions and infantile logic, 20

INDEX

- hope and, 93
- pathological narcissism, 134
- pre-conceptual trauma and, 171
- structure of, 130
- unconscious strategies, 83

U

Ulcerative colitis, 77
Unconscious longing, 140
Unconscious vitality, xviii
Unresolved mourning, 151
Un-thought thoughts, 13, 44, 181, 182
Uranus, 111

V

Vengeful hope, 44, 57, 83, 84, 92, 101, 102, 106, 109
- basic delusion and, 98

Vulnerability, 15

W

Waiting for Godot, 138–144, 151. *See also Beckett, Samuel*
Wild thoughts, 1, 55, 180–184
Winnicott, Donald, xi, 48